HE CALLED ME
ARIELLE

CHAMATHKA GAMAGE

First published in Sri Lanka by
The Jam Fruit Tree Publications

First Edition: April 2020

ISBN: 978-624-95996-0-4

Cover design, typesetting and layout by Jeremy Muller

Printed and bound in Sri Lanka by
The Jam Fruit Tree Publications

The Jam Fruit Tree Publications
A Division of
Addictive International (Pvt) Ltd
366/1 Galle Road, Colombo 00300, Sri Lanka
Tel.: +94 72 726 8078 | E-mail: vjmuller@gmail.com

Dedication

To my dearest students. To my darling friends. To my readers near and far.
If you've gone through fires and you've fought giants.
If you wanted to give up, wondering whether the battle is worth it...
I wanted to tell you...
It's worth it. Keep fighting.
Keep holding on. Things will change.
Your life is worth it. You matter.
No matter what, Don't give up.
And last but never ever the least,

To Ashan,

The boy with a sweet smile,
Who played table tennis with me when I had no clue how,
Who gave me a ride home in the cold winter evening...
In a land far from home,
Waving goodbye with a warm smile...
That made me feel I was back home...
Little did I know, that it was the last I'd ever see you again.
I knew you briefly.
BUT in that time,
You made me feel like I had a friend, when I thought I had none...
You gave hope and joy to me, at a time when life was dark.
You were a light.

I wish you didn't give up.
I wish the world was kinder to you.
I wish I wrote this, before you breathed your last,
Before that light was snuffed out.
Then perhaps, you might still live.
Perhaps we'd see you smile again...
Wherever you are right now... I hope you see this.
Ashan, my friend...
You're still missed
Your life and radiant light,
Made a huge difference...

Acknowledgments

Bringing a book to life is not a solo achievement. It's a daunting task, one that I never thought I'd ever venture on to do… One that I couldn't have done if it wasn't for the amazing people God brought to my life. This book and its success is just as much yours, as it is mine.

Thank you.

To Lord Jesus Christ, My God and Saviour. This was a story you placed in my heart, that you kept pushing me to write amidst my doubts and life's trials. Thank you for forever being the faithful One, who took me step by step through it all, even when I wanted to give up (despite writing a story about a girl who didn't give up – ah! The irony of it! ☺). Thank you for healing me through writing this book in many ways and giving me all that I needed to bring this book to life. Thank you, Lord!

To my father – who **always** believed in me and my writing… even when I didn't…

To My mother, for her endurance and love, even when we drive each other up the wall. ☺

Thank you to David Brining – the first teacher in my life who saw more in me than I ever did. You encouraged me with my writing, with my English… gave me confidence and pushed me to dream, to reach beyond what I thought capable. Thank you, sir. You're the best!

Thank you to Tanika and Keith Obeyesekere for supporting me at the IOM writing competition when I was doubting if my writing was any good and whether I should write this book or not. Thank you for encouraging me and when my entry got selected, thank you for coming in my parent's place (as my dad was hospitalized and no one else could come).

Thank you to Pastor Bernice Benedict, Priscilla Benedict, Jonathan Benedict and everyone at the Tuesday Prayer group at Trinity Christian

Fellowship, who prayed for this book.

Thank you to Maneesha Benedict and Amenthi Dabare, for reading, giving suggestions for improvements and encouraging me with this book.

Thank you to Jeremy Muller and the Jam Fruit Tree Publications, for proof reading, finalizing the editing, arranging the layout and assisting me immensely with the publishing of this book.

Thank you to Mrs. Dipti Kotian for her kind guidance and instruction in the initial phase of editing this book.

Thank you to Rishani Semasinghe and Dr. Colvin Samarasinghe for encouraging me and helping me get fired up again to keep writing when I was facing particularly challenging experiences.

Thank you to Erandi Narangoda and the Soup Bowl team for the various inspiration and support you gave throughout the journey of making this book come alive.

Thank you to the students of Trust Sanctuary International who showed me the need for this book and inspired me to write it. Also thank you to the children who kept encouraging me, warming my heart with their sweet little ways, for being some of the best, supportive students a teacher could dream of having... even after I stopped teaching. Thank you, kids! You guys are awesome!

And last but NEVER EVER the least,

Thank you to Shihanthi De Silva, Praveen Bandara, Shauntell Perera, Rakitha Kuruppu, Amanda Shannon, Lucky Malcolm, Monica & Edward Naumann, Mevan Dissanayake, Angelo Samarawickrema, Piya Singleton, Samira Perera, Nilakshi Premathilaka, Indee Thotawattage, Kushlani W., Nilusha De Silva and everyone else who prayed for me, encouraged me, inspired me and supported me in some way or the other, as I wrote this book and went through the long journey of publishing this book. There were times I doubted myself, times I didn't see the point, times I almost gave up or got lazy... each time, one of you'll pushed me forward. Thank you!

Again, a huge shout out and thank you to ALL of you.

Without you, this book would not have seen the light of day. From the bottom of my heart, Thank you!

CHAPTER ONE

"Now, now girls! Get ready... she's almost here!" Sharlene hurriedly gathered the little girls together in the Rosemary Orphanage for Young Girls.

Situated in Avissawella, the cooler, much greener part of the Colombo district, Rosemary Orphanage sheltered twenty girls, all of them abandoned by their parents at a young age. Sharlene De Silva was the administrator of this orphanage and loved her work – even if, at times, the less than delightful task of dealing with pubescent young women made her want to tear her hair out. Greying hair at that! Despite being only thirty, the strain of her much-loved job was showing. The girls would crack jokes at her expense… their dear stout Ms. Sharlene who stood a couple of inches shorter than some of the girls in her care!

"Is she really all that?" Jayani mumbled – just loud enough for Sharlene to hear.

Counting to ten in her head, Sharlene explained to Jayani for the umpteenth time that Arielle Davidson was their biggest contributor – without her they wouldn't be able to keep the orphanage running.

She held back from declaring that Ms. Davidson was a world-famous philanthropist, extremely gifted in the arts, whose music drew people in, touching their hearts and souls. Sharlene usually kept her distance from these celebrity 'donors' because they were usually after the good publicity it brought them instead of actually caring about the children in the orphanage. Ms. Arielle Davidson was different.

She donated most of her income from her music to support orphanages and low-income single parent families. And that was not all, she actually made an effort to regularly visit the places where she gave her contributions to and took a genuine interest in the children, or so it seemed to Sharlene.

The sound of the doorbell broke Sharlene free from her momentary reverie.

"That must be HER!" she fumbled around excitedly, searching for the bouquet of flowers that the children had gathered from the garden.

"Here you go, Ms. Sharlene," Jayani timidly handed her the bouquet.

Looking kindly at Jayani, Sharlene forgot her earlier annoyance with her.

"I suppose the child has some use..." she thought as she hurried to open the door and welcome Ms. Davidson to their orphanage.

Standing outside the porch of Rosemary Orphanage for Young Girls, Arielle took a deep breath. Her jet-black curls swayed as a breeze brought in the smell of spicy dhal curry from a nearby opened window.

The big whitewashed old brick and mortar building looked

inviting and there were birds perched on a nearby tree, singing in harmony. Butterflies fluttered to and fro in the wide front lawn that needed a bit of mowing. The sun was shining bright in the cloudless sky and Arielle felt her skin burn a little. She inherited her mother's rather fair skin that was prone to sun burn. Arielle shielded her dark eyes from the glare as she looked around her and took another deep breath. Rosemary was, by far, the least formidable institution she'd been to, yet it always made her a little nervous before she entered into any orphanage. Past memories sometimes threatened to flood in and take control of her emotions. As the bronze doorknob turned, Arielle took another deep breath; she was in the middle of muttering her usual power verse to herself: "I can do all things through…" when she was cut off by the loud exclamation of her name.

"Ms. Arielle Davidson!!! Welcome to Rosemary's!!!", Sharlene greeted her with a cheery smile. Suddenly a bouquet of lilies and chrysanthemums thrown in together, blocked Arielle's vision of Sharlene's pearly whites.

The scent of the flowers was a little overwhelming to her at that moment.

"The children gathered them this morning for you. They're so excited to see you!"

"Oh! How delightful! I love lilies!" Arielle remarked as she stepped into the brightly lit hallway, trying to keep her nerves under control.

"They're in the auditorium," Sharlene giggled excitedly.

"Auditorium? Whatever for? I thought we're meeting in the living room like usual?"

"No, Ms. Davidson! This is the first Christmas you're celebrating with us, so the children put together a small performance for you. They wanted to show you how grateful we are to your continued support for our establishment".

Arielle's face lit up.

"Really? What are they performing?"

"It's a surprise!" Sharlene grinned as she led Arielle to the auditorium.

The auditorium was small and whitewashed, like rest of the building, with some wooden chairs lined up to face a small wooden stage. Usually the room was plain and void of any excitement but the children – surely under the influence of Sharlene, no doubt, had outdone themselves with the Christmas decorations.

There was a Christmas tree made out of jam jars wrapped in green tissue paper, lit up by tiny candles placed inside. There were fairy lights, balloons and various colourful Christmas drawings adorning the wall. The atmosphere was definitely festive.

The children started singing Christmas carols as her gaze stopped at the stage.

Sharlene led her to a nearby wooden chair and Arielle settled into be enthralled by the sweet harmony of this little choir.

"Hark the herald angels sing, glory to the new born King..." they finished.

Sharlene stepped onto the stage to make an announcement.

"Now, Ms. Davidson, allow me to present a duet of your song 'Don't Give Up' by Sarah and the newest addition to our little family: Jayani!"

All the children clapped along with Arielle who was excited to see how these two children would sing one of the very first songs she released.

Sarah, dressed in a beautiful baby blue chiffon dress climbed up the stage, with her blonde hair neatly tied by a blue ribbon. A shorter girl who was hiding her face with her hands followed her.

'So that's Jayani...' Arielle thought as she observed the little girl in pink.

She shuffled next to Sarah, clearly uncomfortable. "Will she be okay?" Arielle whispered to Sharlene who came and stood next to her after the announcement.

"I'm actually not sure... Jayani's got a bit of a history," Sharlene whispered back.

Her curiosity rising, Arielle focused on Jayani.

Sarah had started to sing and during the chorus as Jayani joined in, Arielle was pleasantly surprised by Jayani's voice – it sounded as pure as the sound of a ringing bell... clear and resounding.

Jayani still had one hand covering her face as she sang with Sarah.

The music shifted to the second set of verse, which was to be sung by Jayani. Arielle leaned in with anticipation but was disappointed when Jayani made no sound. Her cue came and went and Sarah, looking alarmed, glanced at Sharlene and then nudged Jayani who seemed frozen on stage.

"Sharlene, stop the music! It was a lovely performance... but I think the children are too tired..." Arielle tried to ease the situation.

Suddenly Jayani dashed out of the stage with a loud wail.

"Here she goes again," Sharlene muttered.

"What's that?" Arielle asked.

"Jayani... She's a bit different"

"Clearly! She's an amazing singer! Her voice is so clear and pure… like an angel!" Arielle gushed in admiration.

"That's not what I meant," Sharlene clarified. "Jayani was bullied by some older children at the orphanage she was at before. She tried to run away and was transferred to ours by her concerned guardians."

"Oh really?" Arielle was surprised to hear this about Jayani. She was short, but she looked healthy and was pretty with her dark curly hair.

"Why was she bullied? She seems normal to me…"

"Some of the older children got jealous of her ability to sing. They used to have annual musicals and Jayani kept getting the lead roles. That didn't sit well with some of them so they humiliated her by throwing rotten eggs at her during one of the musicals and taunting her ever since."

"Oh! The poor child!" Arielle felt deeply for Jayani. "She must have felt so hurt!"

Arielle suppressed flash backs from her own past that threatened to resurface.

"Would you mind if I talk to her?" Arielle asked.

"Sure. You can try… but Ms. Davidson, I don't think you'll get through to her… I mean, I know you're used to getting things your way, but this kid… she's as stubborn as a mule".

"Let me try… I can relate to her."

"But Ms. Davidson… you? How?" Sharlene was confused. "You're the daughter of Mr. David Harold Rodrigo – the wealthiest man in the country after the President and Prime Minister! I've heard that you were privately tutored and home-schooled without ever going to a public school… how could you possibly understand Jayani's pain?"

"Please?"

"Fine..." Sharlene relented "She's probably in the backyard swing. That's her usual hideout."

"Thanks," Arielle said hurriedly as she quickly headed towards the door.

Watching Ms. Davidson leave, Sharlene wondered out loud, "There must be more to her past than we know." Unknown to Sharlene, Sarah had been listening to the whole conversation and chimed in, "You're not going to go and eavesdrop now are you Ms. Sharlene?"

Sharlene looked shocked, even though the idea did cross her mind, and she chided Sarah for being silly and walked her to her room – just to make sure 'she' wouldn't eavesdrop.

"I hope it goes well..." Sharlene sighed, looking out at the backyard where she could barely see the figures of Jayani and Arielle.

It was very pretty – the butterfly... with colourful red and black wings, fluttering about the backyard, flying without a care in the world from one flower bed to the next. The sweet aroma of the flowers clearly attracted the butterfly.

Jayani looked at it longingly as she sat alone on the metal swing.

The backyard is the only bit of private space found in the orphanage. It's closed off from the outside world by a brick wall that the painters had not bothered to white wash like the rest of the orphanage. It was where the laundry was generally hung in the mornings and no one came there except when it was time to tend to the flowerbeds.

The swing creaked as Jayani leaned forward. It was an old,

rusty swing that the other girls generally avoided out of fear of breaking it or falling off and hurting themselves. Patches of grass and weeds grew around it so Jayani wasn't scared. She knew the grass would cushion her fall.

Another butterfly fluttered into her view. This one was yellow with black and white spots adorning its wings. It hovered a little before settling on a flower.

"Why can't I be free like them?" she sighed, wiping away the tears that rolled down her cheeks.

'If I could only stop seeing them staring,' she thought as she recalled – again – the familiar scene that haunted her, not only in her dreams but also in reality.

Whenever Jayani stood in front of a large audience, the same scene began to play in front of her eyes.

"Will it ever stop?" she sighed sadly.

"Will what ever stop?" a voice behind her asked. Jayani stood up straight, getting off the swing hurriedly to face the voice. She was startled to see Ms. Arielle before her. She thought it was one of the older girls, coming to taunt her like all the others at the previous orphanage.

"Are you okay?" Ms. Arielle asked her kindly, realizing that she had startled Jayani.

'She's beautiful; much more beautiful in person than on TV,' Jayani thought as she took in the sight of Ms. Arielle Davidson.

Earlier, on stage, Jayani was too panicked to notice anyone. It took all her strength to sing along with the others.

'Ms. Arielle is not beautiful in the super model way' Jayani thought. She's not thin like them with their bony faces. There's just something about her that makes her beautiful. It's almost like there's a glow that makes her shine. Jayani couldn't really understand it.

"Jayani?" Ms. Arielle's voice cut into her thoughts.

"Yes, Ms. Arielle?"

"I was asking if you were okay?"

Jayani looked down at her feet and shrugged, not knowing what to say. She decided to play with a pebble near her toe.

Ms. Arielle waited a little, giving time for Jayani to talk. She kept playing with the pebble.

"Hey, if you'd like to talk to someone, I'm good at listening," Ms. Arielle spoke gently and her voice soothed Jayani.

Finally, Jayani looked up, losing interest in the pebble.

"It doesn't matter. You probably have better things to do, Ms. Arielle. Besides, you wouldn't understand. No one does." Jayani struggled to hold back her tears.

"Try me!"

"You won't! I've talked to some grownups... they all say they understand but, in the end, they all just get angry with me when I can't perform like they want me to! I'm useless! I wish I was never born!" Jayani started sobbing.

That's when something quite out of the ordinary happened!

To Jayani's surprise, Ms. Arielle gathered her into a warm hug.

In her shock, Jayani stopped crying.

"You hugged me!"

"Shouldn't I have? Wait! Don't tell me you hate hugs!"

"No..." Jayani mumbled, suddenly feeling very shy. "It's not that I hate hugs..."

"Then?"

"It's just no one's actually given me a hug before!"

"Ever?" Ms. Arielle looked shocked.

"Ever..." Jayani whispered looking down. "Do you really want me to tell you?" she asked Ms. Arielle.

"Yes, I do Jayani. I want to know what's keeping you from singing with that beautiful voice you have."

"You think my voice is beautiful?"

"Just like an angel's, I'm sure! It's definitely a God given gift."

Jayani's face darkened. "God? Is there really a God?"

"Jayani! Of course there is! Why would you think otherwise?"

"If... If God were real... then he must hate me," Jayani whispered, looking at her feet again.

"Now, why would you say that Jayani? God doesn't hate you. God loves you! He sent Jesus to die on the cross to save you. That's what Christmas and all those carols you sang were all about!"

Anger suddenly flared up in her and Jayani couldn't help bursting out, "If he came to save me, then why didn't he save me from those bullies?"

"The ones who threw rotten eggs at you?" Arielle asked her gently.

"How do you...?"

"Ms Sharlene told me because I was worried about you."

"So you know the reason then."

"I know what happened that time, but I don't know what's keeping you from singing on stage Jayani."

"It's just... I keep seeing them! Every time I'm in front of a crowd or an audience, I see their eyes – full of hatred, their mouths, sneering at me and taunting me... throwing those rotten eggs straight at me. It paralysed me! I couldn't move let alone sing!"

"You're afraid it will happen again?"

"Yeah. I guess."

"It won't! Not everyone's like them. You just have to trust your new audience and push those mean bullies out of your mind. They won over you that day on stage... but don't let them win in your mind too!"

"I wish I was like you Ms. Arielle! You're confident and brave. You're not scared of all those people."

"Well actually, there was a time I was just like you: shy, timid and very afraid".

"What? Ms. Arielle – You?"

"Yeah!!" Looking around to make sure no one else is listening, Ms. Arielle leaned forward and whispered, "If you promise not to tell anyone, I'll tell you all about it... You see... I wasn't always called Arielle."

Jayani was very excited. This was the first time someone was sharing a secret with her and it was not just anyone – it was this amazing person, Ms. Arielle! She felt honoured and solemnly reassured Ms. Arielle: "I promise!"

"So, this is my story..." Ms. Arielle started.

CHAPTER TWO

"I CAN'T STAND HER! I don't want her in this house!" the woman shouted at her husband, her pale face red with anger.

"Rose, honey... she's our daughter. We can't just throw her out." Priyan Wickramasinghe tried to reason with his angry wife.

This was another one of their heated arguments over their daughter. Sometimes he wondered why she was ever born to them.

"Priyan, she's the reason I lost my contract! My life is ruined now because I had to give birth to HER!" Rose continued to shout while tying her long straight hair into a ponytail. The light seemed to bounce off of her jet-black hair. It was silky smooth and well maintained.

"But..." Priyan tried to interrupt his angry wife. He towered over her, but she was never intimidated by him. His curly hair, warm brown eyes and round face hinted at his gentle nature.

"LOOK AT US! We're bimbos!" Rose glared with her coal black eyes gleaming. "We barely have any money to live! I'm sick and tired of trying to scrape by. I'm NOT made for this!"

Priyan looked around their bedroom. Their house wasn't run

down nor was it shabby. Rose got him to get a new paint job done just last month. She wanted the outside walls of the two-storey house to be painted white because it looked classier in her eyes, than its original green colour. The inner walls of the two upstairs bedrooms, the living room and the kitchen downstairs were painted baby blue, the floor carpeted in dark blue with white fluffy rugs in each room. The house was clean and well maintained. Rose made sure of that. They weren't very rich but Priyan made sure Rose didn't have to suffer without the things she wanted. He always tried his best to keep her happy – even if it meant borrowing second hand goods from neighbours and friends.

"Honey, things will change."

He tried to placate her as he always does. He knew she wanted more, and he wished he could provide.

"WHEN?! You said that when we got married but you can't even get a decent job! You got me pregnant with that... that horrid child and now LOOK at me! ME! People used to 'know' me... they used to play my songs in cafes and I used to get fan mail, Priyan! Now the only letters I get are those wretched bills and loan payment notices. I can't live like this anymore. She stole my life from me." Rose, sobbing and exhausted, sank on to the bed.

Priyan felt his heart sink. He hated seeing her cry. He sat next to her and put his arm around her gently.

"Rose, she's our daughter. Let's just be calm and..."

"CALM?! You want me to be CALM?" Rose sharply turned to face him, shrugging his arm off her. "Do you know my worst enemy – that horrid woman Lara got herself a 'little' birthday gift!"

Priyan ignored the stab he felt in his heart. "Darling, what's bad about getting yourself a little birthday gift?"

"You IDIOT! Which world were you in? It's all over the news! She bought the mansion in Venice that was contracted for ME! I gave the order to build it! I was supposed to live there, and I would have if you didn't get me pregnant and we had to marry to avoid scandal. Because of you and this stupid child, they cancelled my contract!"

Priyan reached over and grabbed her hand, "But Rose, you love me.... right? I mean is it that bad?"

There was a moment of silence; A moment that seemed to stretch too long.

For the second time, Rose shrugged his hand away from her.

"Love? No, Priyan... I don't think I love you" Rose whispered as the truth dawned on her. "I don't love you or that dimwit of a child! In fact, I HATE your guts. BOTH of you... ESPECIALLY that child! You wouldn't even get rid of her for me!"

Priyan looked taken aback. The knife that stabbed his heart seemed to turn in its spot, making the pain worse. The argument had escalated to a new level. This was the first time she said she hated him. Usually it was the child.

He loved children and especially his own little one, so how could he throw her out the way Rose wanted him to... but hearing her accusations he started wondering if he made a huge mistake. 'The child is slow...' he thought to himself but suddenly his thoughts were interrupted as he saw a sharp gleam in his wife's eyes. It disturbed him, and his instincts took over.

"Whatever you're thinking of... DON'T do it!"

Rose laughed manically. It scared him to see her this way.

"You can't tell me what to do! I am DONE with you and this dump! I QUIT!"

"What do you mean you quit Rose?"

She didn't answer but instead turned around and took her suitcase from under the bed. She hastily started to fill it up with her clothes while all Priyan could do was watch – frozen from the horror of it all. Then, she took her phone out and called a taxi.

Slowly, the reality of the situation dawned on him. The truth of what was happening unfroze him and he reached out to stop her from leaving.

"DON'T touch me! Don't call me. Don't text me. We are done! If you still love me, you'll let me leave. I'm done!"

She grabbed the suitcase and kicked the slightly opened door wide open.

She looked straight ahead at the new life she could lead as a single woman in the music industry and she walked out the front door.

Priyan miserably followed her, trying to reason with her to no avail.

Rose stomped down the staircase, opened the front door and stood at the porch, waiting for her taxi.

"Rose... please don't do this," Priyan tried to change her mind.

Rose glared at the man she married. The man she gave up her dreams for. He was still handsome, despite the few lines that had appeared near the corner of his. Before she could change her mind, the Kangaroo cab pulled up, the driver honking his horn.

Rose hesitated for just one split second, then shook off any last-minute regrets and got in the taxi, closed the door and she was gone.

Rose had left the house.

There was stillness in her wake, interrupted only by the sobs of the broken man who slid down the front porch, leaning against the wooden door, as all strength finally left him.

Priyan worshiped Rose. He adored her and loved her greatly. He withstood all her insults, criticisms and grumblings because he couldn't imagine the emptiness of life without her... but now, she was gone.

In the shadows near the bedroom, huddled in a corner, little six-year-old Heather saw and heard it all. Her little chubby cheeks were streaked with tears and her black curly hair was in a crow's nest of a mess.

She had seen her mom stride past her, her father following her steps without seeing Heather standing there, shocked at the words she heard.

Heather knew her mom didn't like her very much. Rose never liked to spend time with her and even when they went to the park, she never got hugs and kisses like the other kids got from their moms. Rose barely paid any attention to her, but Heather never thought her mom could hate her. She didn't think it was possible.

She never knew that she was the reason for all the fights and problems her family was going through. Her little heart felt heavy, like a giant rock was tied to it and was weighing it down. She followed her parents silently and watched through the opened door as the taxi pulled in, her mother got in and left them... without a word of goodbye to her. She saw her father crumbling to the ground in tears.

"All this, because of me?"

Heather regretted the day she was born.

CHAPTER THREE

"Heather!" Priyan shouted again from the kitchen. "Where's that stupid child?" he muttered to himself.

It was two years since Rose left and they hadn't heard from her since. Priyan had decided not to pursue her, not only for his sake and Heather's. He let her go, to allow her to pursue her music. He felt it was the least he could do for her. He blamed himself for being the reason Rose lost her former glory. The guilt never left him. If only they didn't have this useless child, things would have turned out so differently. Rose could have lived in her beautiful house in Venice and I could have been with her. I could have gotten a permanent job and then married her once we had enough money, but no! Heather was born, and it ruined everything!

Simmering anger returned Priyan to reality. It was 7:00 a.m. and she was asleep!

Since Rose left, a neighbour – Shriyani Peiris, came in the mornings to take care of Heather. Shriyani was unemployed and did not have children. She was generally free and so, she kindly offered to help. She took Heather to school because Priyan left for work by 6:45.

A week ago, Shriyani left town to visit her family in Kandy. She moved to their neighbourhood in Dehiwela sometime after Priyan moved in with Rose, because her husband was employed at the Bank of Ceylon in Dehiwela. But for now, she was gone, so Priyan asked his younger brother Charith for help.

Charith Wickramasinghe did odd jobs here and there but was luckily free for the coming weeks. He had a problem with alcohol and a wandering eye, so for the longest time Priyan avoided Charith. He didn't let Charith visit when Rose was around. 'She was too special to be exposed to this scum,' he thought – but with Heather, he consoled himself thinking that 'there was no choice since Shriyani was far away in Kandy'. So, for the last three days Charith came over. Priyan shrugged off any misgivings when the doorbell rang, announcing Charith's arrival.

"Heather! Uncle Charith is here! I'm leaving!" Priyan shouted, angry again at the child's tardiness.

Priyan opened the door and the stench of alcohol greeted him along with Charith's dishevelled appearance. Priyan was tall but Charith dwarfed him in height.

"Don't judge. Long night" Charith smiled with crazed eyes, as Priyan was about to question him. His face was sharp and thin, unlike Priyan's, with the shadow of a beard. He had short, unkempt hair that he ran his fingers through every time he smiled or grinned.

Priyan sighed at his brother's lifestyle and gave the extra keys to Charith. He rushed out to catch the train, shouting one last instruction: "Don't forget to pick her up at two!"

Charith's eyes shone as he replied, "Don't worry! I won't forget."

He watched Priyan dash across the street. Safely out of sight,

Charith decided it was time to start the operation he was waiting to try, ever since he started babysitting. He locked the front door of the house and made sure all the curtains were drawn. Then he slowly made his way to Heather's room with the keys finally in his hands.

He couldn't believe his luck! All he did was complain about Heather making him late for an appointment. He said she wouldn't come out of her room for school and Priyan agreed to give the key. Charith couldn't believe that Heather kept quiet about him. She had not spoken to Priyan.

"Well... works out for me... but not for you darling!" he muttered as he raised his hand to knock on her door.

"Knock, Knock, Knock"

The sound sent chills up eight-year-old Heather's spine.

"Heather! It's uncle Charith! Open the door..."

Daddy let him come again? Heather wondered in despair.

She was in her PJs, huddled on her bed, covered in her navy-blue Mini Mouse blankets. She didn't want uncle Charith to come inside.

The first day uncle Charith came to take her to school, he hugged her tightly. She couldn't breathe but he wouldn't let go when she tried to break free. Something told her to stay away from him – so she bit his hands, ran into her room and locked herself in.

Since then, she didn't leave her room. Her father didn't seem to notice. No one did. She was scared, alone and hungry but at least uncle Charith couldn't come into her room. It was her safe sanctuary.

He tried to get her to open the door. First, he asked her nicely, but she felt very strongly that she shouldn't open the door. Then he ended up shouting and banging on the door, which scared Heather even more. She decided never to open that door to him. For the last two days she endured the dreaded shouts and threats of what he would do to her, coming from outside her door.

Why is this happening to me? she wondered when the shadows crept up on her, but no one came in search of her. The blue walls of her room reflected her mood. *Why does everyone hate me so much?*

She thanked her lucky stars that the locks on the door held, even with all the banging, so she braced herself to endure his threats today too.

Suddenly, the knocking stopped. It was eerily quiet and the hair on the back of her neck stood up.

Heather sensed something bad was going to happen.

To her horror, she heard a key turning in the lock and, as she peered over her bed sheet, she saw the doorknob turn and the door creak open, revealing the ghastly figure of uncle Charith – with feverish, crazed eyes.

Heather felt a scream escape her as pure terror gripped her.

"No one will come for you now little missy," uncle Charith grinned an evil, twisted grin as he turned to lock the door behind him.

"You know, you look like your mother," he muttered as he struggled to lock the door with shaking hands. He was clearly excited.

"Priyan never let me meet her... thought she was too good for the likes of me... but I guess I'll have you instead!"

Heather was frozen in shock. She didn't understand the sinister meaning behind uncle Charith's words, but she knew in her gut that something bad was going to happen. She wanted to run away but there was no way out. So she opened her mouth again to scream as loud as she could.

"Priyan! You have a call." Sheran, a young man who worked with Priyan, brought the phone to him.

"Who was it?" Priyan wondered as his heart leaped. He hoped that it was Rose.

"Hello?" He answered in anticipation.

"Mr. Priyan?" a man's voice replied to his disappointment.

"Yes. Who is this?"

"I'm calling from the police. There was an incident at your home that concerns your daughter. She's receiving treatment for some minor bruises and trauma. We need you to come in for a statement."

"Heather? What happened to her?"

"We got a report from the shop in front of your house of a young girl screaming. The shop keepers were concerned for your daughter because they haven't seen her come out of the house to go to school for three days. They reported that they saw a strange man going in and out of the house..."

"That would be my brother Charith," Priyan replied hastily. "...but what do you mean she wasn't out for three days? Charith was there to take her to school!"

"Sir, are you seated?"

"No..." Priyan replied perplexed.

"I suggest you sit down"

"Would you get to the point please? What happened to my daughter?"

"When the police arrived at the scene, they found your daughter tied to her bed and your brother attempting to..."

The blood drained from Priyan's face. He barely caught the rest of the sentence.

"I think you've said enough, sir. I'll be there immediately."

"Is everything alright?" Sheran asked with a worried expression as Priyan felt the phone slip out of his hand.

"What have I done?" he whispered.

Sheran looked concerned but was silent. He waited for Priyan to continue but instead, dazed, Priyan grabbed his jacket and dashed out of the office.

Jackson looked at his watch. It was 7:00 a.m. Priyan left the house for work as usual but Jackson didn't see little Heather with him.

Stacking up the empty newspaper stand, Jackson noted that the toffee jar needed a refilling.

"Himalie! Honey, we're out of toffees. Be an angel and bring some out for me, will you?"

"You gave extra to the children this morning too, didn't you?" Himalie giggled and tousled his hair playfully as she brought out more toffees. She loved the way he kept his slightly long straight brown hair like Kimura Takuya in 'Hero' – the J-drama they loved to watch.

Jackson was born to a single parent family. His mother was Japanese, and his father was Australian. They lived in Sydney for a long time, but he never met his father. He moved to Sri Lanka with his mother after she started her own restaurant in Colombo. His mother fell in love with Sri Lanka during a brief vacation with their Australian-Sri Lankan neighbour. He spoke a little Japanese but communicated mostly in English.

Himalie was born to a Sinhalese family. She was tan, slim, with long black hair that she kept in a ponytail. She was a fan of Japanese culture and learned Japanese as a hobby to visit Japan in the future. As fate would have it, Himalie and Jackson met each other at a church in Colombo when they were twenty-five and were happily married for twenty years. They opened their own little shop styled after an Australian convenience store Jackson had fond memories of, which was connected to their small cosy house. Sadly, they were not blessed with children, even though they both would have adored a child of their own. They made peace with it over the years.

Children would take advantage of this love and ask for extra sweets from Jackson on their way to school.

Whenever Heather passed by, it was Jackson's pleasure to give her a little chocolate. She seemed a quiet girl and Jackson has heard the local gossip about her family. He could only imagine the trauma that the girl went through with her parent's separation.

Some weeks back, when Jackson didn't see Heather pass their store for a few days, he was concerned. He talked to Himalie about it. That's when they heard a blood-curdling scream from her house.

They immediately called the police and Jackson dashed across the street to go and check up on the child.

The door of her white washed house was locked but luckily Priyan had given a spare key to their neighbour and close friend Shriyani. Himalie knew where she hid it. It took her only a minute to get it and Jackson was about to walk in when the police jeep arrived.

The officer rushed out and warned them to wait outside. Jackson was about to protest but Himalie held him back.

"Let them do their job, honey"

Jackson's body ached with the effort it took to stay still.

The minutes etched on.

They heard the siren of an ambulance growing louder and then there were footsteps.

"Dear Lord, I hope the girl is okay" Himalie whispered, her fingernails dug into Jackson's arms.

Jackson couldn't bear it any longer. He peered inside – just when one of the officers came outside. He carried Heather in his arms. The girl was pale as a sheet and looked as if she had seen a ghost. Jackson heard Himalie gasp.

"What?"

"Look at her hands!"

Jackson looked and saw ugly black and blue bruises all over her arms.

The siren grew louder, and they watched in silence as the ambulance came into view. The officer gently laid Heather on the stretcher that the ambulance staff pulled out.

The officer spoke softly to one of the paramedics. Jackson inched closer to hear their conversation.

"…She was bound to the bed. We got there just in time to stop that man from molesting her. If we came just minutes later…"

The paramedic shook her head;

"What has this world come to? How can someone try to abuse such a little girl?"

"In our line of work, we sadly see too many of these stories. She looked a bit traumatized and dehydrated. Almost like she hasn't eaten in a while. Take care of her, will you?"

"Yes sir! Looks like there's an audience…we better get going."

The paramedic got in the ambulance and closed the door. The officer busied himself. He cleared out a path for the ambulance as a crowd gathered, drawn by the sight of the police jeep, the flashing lights and loud siren of the ambulance.

Jackson and Himalie watched in silence as the ambulance took Heather away.

Jackson couldn't believe what he was hearing. That strange man he saw going into their house sure was a rotten apple. He clenched his fist.

"If I could get my hands on that son of a …."

Himalie unclenched his fist and distracted him from his angry reverie.

"Don't even think about it!"

"But Himalie… did you hear what happened?"

"Yes… but the police caught him. They'll make sure justice is served."

"I suppose…"

That was the last time they saw Heather for a few weeks.

They heard that she was out of the hospital and back home, but she still hasn't gone back to school.

Jackson kept an eye out for her but as the clock neared 8:00 a.m. he knew it was another day that Heather would miss school.

"Looks like she's missing school today too" Jackson sighed.

"Who? Heather?"

"Yeah... who else?"

"I heard someone working at the clinic say that she's refusing to go to school or step out of her room. The national child protection authorities have got involved."

"Really? So what are they doing?"

"They're getting her to see a therapist from the clinic"

"She's going to miss so much school work."

"I know... and from what I've heard from one of her teachers, she was struggling in class even before this... I don't know how she'd pick up after such a long absence."

"Is there anything we can do to help, Himalie?"

Himalie paused and thought for a moment.

"Actually... I was thinking..."

"What?"

"You know how we both used to tutor during college?"

"You think we should tutor her?"

"Yes! Don't you think that will help her catch up quickly?"

"Well... yes... but how can we get her school material?"

"Remember the teacher I told you about? She comes to our church! I can easily ask her for the material. I'm sure she wouldn't mind sharing, considering the circumstances."

"We might need to talk to Priyan about it."

"You do that!"

"Great! Himalie you're a gem! What would I do without you!"

"That's why you married me!" Himalie grinned.

"Absolutely" Jackson smiled and gave her a quick hug, then he moved to leave.

"Where are you going?"

"I'm going to see Priyan."

"Can't you just call him?"

"No... I want to meet him and talk to him" Jackson was resolute about it.

"Sure... bring something nice from the bakery on your way back."

Jackson smiled in response and waved as he left.

Himalie watched him as he left and smiled to herself.

"God, you've blessed me with a good man. Thank you... Thank you so much!"

CHAPTER FOUR

A*LONE, AGAIN,* HEATHER thought to herself miserably. She was eleven years old now, but nothing much had changed. She still didn't have any friends.

After her ordeal with uncle Charith, she missed school for several months and struggled to catch up with schoolwork. Part of her was afraid of how she would be treated when she went back. Would people know? Would they care? Or would they laugh at her?

Jackson and Himalie from the store in front of her house tutored her during the months she missed school. They continued to help her until her grades improved in each term's exams. Some of her teachers said they were proud of her because she performed better compared with her previous grades – even after the bad experience she went through. It was all thanks to Jackson and Himalie. If it wasn't for their constant help and encouragement, Heather wouldn't have taken a step back into school.

It was hard.

Her classmates whispered behind her back about her frizzy curly hair, how unkempt and fat she was... how she was poor and how her parents were divorced and so on.

They whispered about how they didn't want to be friends with her because none of their parents wanted them to be friends with her. After she got better grades, however, things started to change... especially close to the exam time. Everyone talked to her, offered warm smiles and sweet words until she helped them with their work.

None of them actually cared about her. They just used her because they didn't want to fail in class and get scolded by their parents.

Huddled in their little groups, they giggled and whispered about her – ever so often they glanced her way as if to make sure she wasn't listening.

The truth was, they were not as quiet as they thought they were.

She heard every comment and they stung. It grieved her heart immensely to realize that she was unloved by even her classmates.

Being back at school was not a comforting experience for her... but at least no one talked about her experience with uncle Charith, so Heather had one thing to be glad about.

This year too, she took her usual seat. The plastic chair made no noise against the soft grey carpet. Heather sat in the centre of the class and she did what she always did when she was in class. She took out her favourite novel and started to read – or pretended to at least.

It gave her something to do, something to focus on, other than her lack of friends. It was difficult at first because the whispers and giggles made her nervous and on edge. She felt open and vulnerable. But once the words in the books came into focus, she would read them and sometimes re-read the same page until she was able to shut down the noise around her and enter the story of her book.

The words leapt out at her. The story was about a girl who was called the "lioness". She was brave and fought against enemy warriors. She wished to be like that. Suddenly, a shadow fell on her book.

Looking up, Heather saw Pavani Fonseka's beautiful, smiling face. She wasn't smiling in a mocking way but in fact, kindly.

"Why is Pavani here? Why is she smiling? At me?" Heather thought to herself, surprised at the fact that the most popular girl in her class had approached her.

Pavani was neither too tall nor short. Her skin was olive coloured and her hair effortlessly cascaded on her shoulders like a waterfall. She had a fringe that she maintained at the perfect length and her clothes matched her accessories, perfectly. Pavani was always perfect.

"Sorry... what did you say?" Heather asked Pavani. She was engrossed with her thoughts to the extent that she missed what Pavani said. Heather felt dumb.

"Oh... I just said Hi! Wanted to see how you're doing"

"I'm fine. Thanks" Heather mumbled shyly. She still couldn't believe Pavani came and talked to 'her' directly.

"I was just wondering if you'd want to share what happened to you some time back when we were eight... everyone was really worried about you."

"They were?" Heather wondered out loud, surprised at this new information.

"Of course! You didn't come to school for months! We all wondered what happened to you... we just didn't want to ask you before because the teachers told us not to... but it should be fine now right?"

Heather didn't reply.

"It's just... there's been so many strange stories... we just want to know the truth."

Something shifted in Pavani's eyes as she said this, but Heather wasn't sure. It must have been her imagination.

"Thank you for worrying. It... It means a lot," Heather stammered shyly.

Pavani looked at her kindly and said, "Okay then, at lunch time... come and join us"

"Sure..." Heather mumbled, "Thanks".

Pavani smiled again. "Don't mention it", she said as she walked over to her group of friends who waited for her. Pavani had her back to Heather but she must have said something good about her because all the girls in the group smiled at Heather and returned to their conversations.

Heather turned back to her book. Suddenly, the adventures of the lioness failed in its appeal.

"Pavani just invited me for lunch!? Everyone was worried about me!? Is this true? Was I just assuming and imagining all those negative things?" Heather wondered, confused at the turn of events.

For once in her school life, Heather looked forward to the break.

Ms. Erandi Weerasinghe gathered her books and took one last look at the class. "Don't forget, homework is due tomorrow!"

"Yes Ma'am" the class shouted in unison. They were eager for her to leave the class.

"Thank you, children. See you tomorrow!"

"Thank you, teacher, God bless you!" the students got to their feet and chimed together as was required by school rules.

The minute Ms. Erandi walked out of the class, the dam broke. The order in the classroom vanished as the children sprang out of their chairs. The plastic chairs and desks lost its alignment as a throng of children rushed out of the class. Some played with each other, some ran to the cafeteria to be the first in queue and others took out their lunch, brought from home.

This was usually Heather's cue to take her peanut butter sandwich and leave the classroom in search of a quiet spot in the school garden to eat in peace, away from the whispers. Today was different. Today she was invited to have lunch with Pavani! Pavani! The most popular girl in the class! She was wealthy and perfect in every way. She was good at so many things like sports and even singing. Everyone just flocked around her. The only thing she wasn't number one in was academics because Heather started taking first place. Before she started getting tutored by Jackson and Himalie, Pavani really was the all-round star.

"Hey Heather!" Pavani waved from her seat.

Fighting her nerves, Heather grabbed the brown paper bag with her sandwich and made her way to Pavani.

"Grab your chair and come silly! Where will you sit?"

As heat flushed into her face, Heather knew she was blushing. She quickly grabbed her chair, embarrassed at her mistake.

Pavani shifted to make room for her food on the small plastic desk.

"So... tell me, what exactly happened to you?"

"Well..." Heather started a little hesitantly. Should she really open up and tell her the true story? Pavani was listening intently, as if she was hanging on to every word Heather spoke. She had never received such attention from anyone before.

"You know about my mom and my dad?"

"Yes... I've heard that they are..." Pavani hurriedly looked around to make sure no one else was listening and in a hushed tone said, "they are divorced, right?" scrunching her pretty face to make the word 'divorce' seem distasteful like sour milk.

Heather felt a sinking sensation; a foreboding sense that whispered, "stop talking". But it was too late. Her mouth had a life of its own and continued to speak.

"Well... my uncle Charith was supposed to take me to school for a few days..." Heather told Pavani the entire story.

Pavani listened carefully and took it all in. Heather loved her intent attention. It looked like she actually wanted to hear what she had to say. This was the first time someone other than her teachers 'really' listened to her.

All her teachers loved her because of her good behaviour in class and now, because of her perfect grades... well, except Mrs. Lacey – the grey haired, stocky, math teacher. Mrs. Lacey disliked Heather and always picked on her. Every time there was a difficult sum and Heather struggled, Mrs. Lacey would look over her thick spectacles and seemed to gloat over her struggle. She pointedly announced to the class that even the 'best' are not so great when it came to mathematics, insisting that people weak in Math were not smart.

Heather's music teacher, Miss Chathuri Gunesekera, a tall lady with hair dyed brown, a twinkling laugh and angelic voice, encouraged her when she was down about Mrs. Lacey's remarks. She would say: "Come now Heather, you might not be good at Math, but you are definitely a talented girl! You can sing like a nightingale – so beautifully, you're growing in your piano skills and Mr. David is teaching you Theatre and Art, right?" Heather remembered nodding. "Mr. David said you were a natural actress and your paintings were the best in your grade!"

"Really?" Heather would whisper and hoped these comments were true. She barely dared to believe it.

Then Miss Chathuri would laugh with her twinkling laugh and said "Of course! Now, where's that beautiful smile of yours? Let me see it!"

And then, only after Heather smiled, she would let her go.

"So *that's* what happened," – Pavani broke the silence that settled in, once Heather finished telling her story.

"Yeah..." Heather mumbled.

"I see... well, it's too bad Heather. I wish we could have been friends, but you're clearly not the kind of girl I'd want around me," Pavani said in a sickeningly sweet voice.

It took Heather a moment to process the sudden change in Pavani's tone and manner. She no longer looked at her with sympathy or kindness but condescendingly, in a mocking manner.

"Wha... What do you mean Pavani? *YOU* asked me to come sit with you!"

"So, you thought we're friends? Awww... how cute!" Pavani taunted.

"You were lying? You just wanted to find out what happened?"

the realization dawned on Heather and the pain that came with it cut deep into her.

It made her happy, even if it was for a brief few hours, when she thought she finally had a friend. The pain of betrayal stung her already bruised heart. Suddenly, Pavani stood up and the class went quiet as all eyes turned towards them.

"So, everyone, I know we've all been wondering what happened to Miss goody two shoes here!"

"Yeah!" a few shouted back in response.

"Pavani... Please don't!" Heather managed to croak out when she realized what Pavani was going to do.

"Well, it seems our perfect little angel Heather is not such an angel after all! She's got her uncle seduced!"

The class went quiet for a minute.

Joe – the tallest guy in the class with a face full of freckles wondered aloud "Seduced? What's that?" Everyone else looked equally puzzled.

Heather was the only person other than Pavani whose vocabulary was good enough in their grade to understand what it meant. She heard Pavani grind her teeth in annoyance. "Fool! Heather tried to get her uncle to like her like a boyfriend!"

At this, the whole class gasped, and faces twisted with anger, revolt and disgust stared at Heather.

Heather felt a lump rising in her throat. She was going to cry.

"That's not what happened!" She tried to tell everyone... but it was too late. No one wanted to listen to her.

Everyone huddled together and started whispering all the while, looking at her.

This time, they made it no secret that they were talking about her.

"No wonder her mom left her!" someone muttered.

"Yeah! She acts like she's sooooo good and smart! What a fat liar!"

"My mom always told me not to be friends with kids whose parents are 'divorced'. She said they were 'troubled'" Joe spoke loud for everyone to hear.

Charitha, who's eldest sister was a tennis champion in the 12th grade looked pointedly at Heather and remarked out loud, "I've heard my sister call girls like *HER* sluts!"

"Let's call her that!" Joe sneered and as Pavani gleefully taunted, "Fat Heather is a slut!" the whole class joined in.

Tears streamed down Heather's face.

"Don't they know what it means? I'm not a slut. This is so unfair! I didn't do anything wrong!"

The taunts continued as Heather gathered her food and ran out of the class thinking, "I'm never going back there again..."

"Heather? There you are!"

Heather looked up with eyes red with crying, her hair messier than usual and face blotched with tears.

Mr. David Brodin was startled. He was tall with dark brown hair and hazel eyes. With his black-rimmed glasses, he looked a little bit like an older version of Harry Potter according to some of his students who were avid fans of the series. His fair British skin was not used to the harsh Sri Lankan sun. He burnt easily and would turn red like a lobster. It was not his habit to venture outside when it was hot and sunny, but this time was an exception.

Heather was one of his favourite students (even though he knew as a teacher he's not supposed to have favourites). With Heather it was difficult not to like her. She was well mannered, obedient and responsive in class – always improving and performing excellently. He never saw her this upset although Miss Chathuri had mentioned that things were not easy for Heather.

"Mr. David!!!" Heather sprung to her feet and hastily wiped off her tears.

The small herbs garden behind the cafeteria was usually empty. Heather didn't think anyone could find her here. She was embarrassed.

Mr. David gave her few minutes to collect herself.

"Young lady, it's the last class before the final school bell rings. You were not in class."

It was a statement. Not a question.

Heather nodded, looking down at her feet.

"What happened? You're not usually the kind of student who skips class."

"Oh! Mr. David!" Heather sobbed, and she told him what happened. Mr. David looked hard at Heather through his glasses. "I'll have a chat with Pavani and the others about this," he finally said. He knew Heather wouldn't make up a story like this.

"Please sir. If you don't mind, could you keep it to yourself? They'll just make a bigger fuss..."

"Well... what are you planning to do about this?" Mr. David asked truly concerned about this child.

It's not uncommon for students to go down wrong paths because of experiences like this. He felt like Heather might be facing a fork in her road. The wrong decision would lead her down a path full of regrets and David felt it was his duty as a teacher to do all within his power to guide her right.

"I don't know sir. I was thinking of quitting school. I'd go home, my dad doesn't care anyway... so I'll just pretend I'm going to school but go somewhere else... maybe to the library."

This was exactly the kind of thing David wanted to prevent.

Heather was a brilliant, talented student with great potential. He would not let her quit school without a fight.

Looking intently at Heather, David spoke softly "Heather, I know things are difficult for you at school, at home – everywhere, really... but quitting is not the best answer to your problem."

"But sir... what else can I do? How can I face everyone?"

"I've heard a famous quote that says, 'Courage is not about being fearless but choosing to do the right thing even when you're afraid.' So, Heather, don't give up. Take courage. If you give up, you're giving them the victory. The only way you can defeat them is by showing up and doing your best – even when they're putting you down. With time, they'll see how wrong they were about you."

Heather smiled weakly.

"I'm here for you if you need anything... okay?"

Tears clouded Heather's vision and before she could stop herself, she blurted out "Sir! I wish I had a father like you!"

Mr. David was touched. He didn't expect such a reaction from Heather.

He grinned and patted her head. "So, are we ready to go back to class?"

"Yes Sir!"

"Mrs. Lacey said your notes will be incomplete since you skipped class."

"Yes sir... I need to borrow someone's books to complete them"

"Who will you ask from?"

"I don't know sir. I don't know if anyone would give me their books now..."

"Let's see if I could help"

They walked into the classroom and Mr. David excused himself from Miss Chathuri who was teaching at the time.

"Oh! Thank God you found her!"

Miss Chathuri remarked in relief as she saw Heather.

The entire class snickered as Heather came into view, hair dishevelled, eyes red and face blotched with tears. She must have looked like a wild child.

Miss Chathuri gave her a tissue and gently guided her to her chair.

Mr. David stared silently at the class. His face-hardened and lips set in a firm, grim tone.

Soon the class settled into silence. Mr. David spoke softly.

"Is there anyone in this class who'd like to explain what happened today?"

No one responded.

Mr. David's tone was calm, yet it was so different from his usual jovial tone – everyone immediately knew they should not mess with him.

"Well... in the future, I hope such things will not happen in this class. If it does, the entire class can expect detention until the end of the school year"

The whole class groaned in unison.

"I'm serious about this" David stressed. "Now, is there anyone who'd like to share their notes with Heather? She missed quite a lot of class work"

"Excuse me Sir," Pavani politely raised her hand, seeking permission to speak.

David nodded, granting her permission.

"Heather is the smartest in the class. She's always first. She can study the textbooks and I'm sure she'll still score well because she's so brilliant. I'm sure of it, Sir! It's not like that for us Sir... we need our notes every day to study. Otherwise we won't do well for our exams. Would you like that Sir?"

David was stricken by the malice Pavani showed towards Heather. There was so much manipulation and meanness in such a beautiful little girl. Truly, outward appearances spoke nothing of inner character.

David looked at Miss Chathuri and she understood the plan that brewed in his mind. She nodded in agreement.

"Well then, does this mean no one is willing to give Heather their notes?"

Everyone nodded in agreement.

Heather's eyes caught hold of David's, with tears swelling up again. Full of compassion towards her, David made his decision.

"Well then, you won't have any complaints if the teachers give our notes to Heather directly."

At this the entire class groaned.

Heather couldn't dare to believe this turn of events. She looked at Mr. David and then at Miss Chathuri. They both smiled at her with the most loving smiles she had ever received in her life. Heather's heart warmed, and her eyes lit up. Hope was kindled. Even if her classmates hated her, she wasn't alone. She had her teachers' support. She would stay and fight this battle – just like Mr. David advised.

"I'm not giving up!" she murmured.

CHAPTER FIVE

It was August 2006. A few months back the monsoon rains stopped so the land was hot and humid. Heather usually hated this season, but this year was different. She waited in excitement, seated in the air-conditioned auditorium of her high school.

A few days earlier, there was an announcement about selections for the end-of-the-year school play. It was the musical *Cinderella* and Heather was excited to try out for the lead role – or any other.

She just wanted to be a part of the play no matter the role. Heather remembered the times Ms. Chathuri in her previous school complimented her voice; she said it was beautiful. Dear Mr. David also treated her as the star actress in class. She was confident she'd get at least a minor role in the play.

The entire atmosphere of the dimly lit auditorium buzzed with excitement. The only bright light in the hall was the spotlight, highlighting the stage. Hopeful students, one by one, occupied the green leather seats as the seniors allowed them in to audition. Since the drama club organized the play, the senior students were responsible for selections. Mrs. Murray – the senior school's theatre department teacher in charge, was available to offer guidance but the final choice of selections was at the hands of a panel of three seniors running the drama club for that academic year.

Heather was anxious for her turn. Waiting was the hard part. Once on stage, she would shine but until her feet hit the stage, she was Heather – scared and nervous Heather. When she took the stage Heather would no longer be herself. She wouldn't just 'act' her character; she had the ability to 'become' her character. She would feel the emotions of her character and forget that she was fat, frizzy haired, Heather who was unwanted and unnoticed by everyone. That's what she loved about theatre. For the few minutes on stage – she would be someone else – someone powerful, someone courageous, and someone who had a meaningful part to play in a story – someone who was noticed.

Sometimes she wished her reality would be like that – where she was wanted, noticed and had some important part to play but unfortunately, that was not the case. Her father barely came home or took any notice of her unless the report card needed to be signed. Then he would pay attention to her because he wanted to make sure he could boast that she got good grades to anyone who'd bother to ask how she performed at school.

He took pride in the fact that Heather was enrolled at a good school in the outskirts of Colombo. Sending her to Oceans International was a dream come true to him because it was one of the leading international schools in the province. It was an expensive school and, without the scholarship Heather received for her good grades, her father would not have been able to afford it. However, he had conveniently forgotten this and pridefully boasted to his family and friends about his ability to financially support Heather's education at Oceans.

In her new class even though the kids were different from her previous school, Heather was unable to make any friends. How could she trust anyone? She didn't want to go through the same pain of betrayal and shame she endured in her previous school. She wanted it to be a thing of the past – so she kept her head down, avoided eye contact and just stayed invisible in the class. Everyone seemed to be fine with that – they didn't bother her or disturb her – and for that she was grateful.

"Number 200" – Janath, one of the seniors in the panel shouted above the chatter in the auditorium.

That's my number! Heather realized and quickly fumbled out of her seat and dashed to the front.

"What's your name?" Janath asked her, while he sized her up with his eyes.

"Heather," she replied.

"Okay Heather, go on stage"

She obeyed quickly and walked to the spot light at the centre of the stage, in the same manner as others before her.

"You wanted to audition for... Cinderella?" an astonished voice questioned from the panel.

It was Bella Van Asbeck – the star of the previous year's play. She was reading through Heather's form. Her large expressive eyes squinted in the dim light of the auditorium and her small pink lips was set in a grim line.

Bella was beautiful. She was fair with clear skin that seemed to glow under the auditorium's dim fluorescent light. Her ancestors from her father's side were barons in the Netherlands according to school gossip. She was slim and had long straight hair that she kept tied in a single dainty braid.

Bella cleared her throat and Heather realized she was waiting for her to answer.

"Y...Yes..." Heather stuttered, with flushed cheeks. She was too distracted. They must have thought she was stupid to try for Cinderella.

"Actually... I don't mind any role... I just want to be part of the play"

"Sure doll," Damien Silva said kindly. He was the president of the drama club. He was tan, stocky and muscular in built. "Let's see what you got. Can you read out the second act and sing the song at the end?"

"Sure".

"Okay... the stage is all yours" Damien announced. This line signalled for quiet in the hall as she performed.

Heather felt her mouth drying up as she gazed at the eyes staring at her from the seats. For a minute she was overwhelmed with the memory of the time she stood in front of her classroom while everyone snickered.

"Get a grip, Heather. You need to ace this." She thought to herself. "You're not Heather. You are Cinderella".

And she took one last glance at the audience before she became Cinderella.

Bella glared with increasing unease as Heather performed.

"She's good," Janath Goonatilake whispered – always the first to comment.

"Wow! That voice!" Damien muttered.

The boys seemed enthralled by her performance.

"Were they blind?" Bella thought to herself.

Pointing at Heather, out loud Bella said, "She's fat! Cinderella has to be thin... at least thinner than *that!*" Pausing for effect – and for the point to sink in, Bella then continued, "She can't get this part. You know that!"

She sensed Damien sigh next to her.

"I know. What a waste of such a good voice"

"She's talented for sure," Janath agreed.

"I suppose her acting is good," Bella agreed half-heartedly.

She couldn't believe 'she' was feeling threatened by this ugly, fat kid, but the boys were right – Heather was a talented actress. If she was slimmer – she would really be a serious threat to Bella's position in school as the star actress.

"Can we give her a different role?" Damien wondered.

"You can't!" Mrs. Murray interrupted with a sigh.

They forgot she was even there.

"Why ever not?" the boys exclaimed together.

"Her voice is too pure and beautiful. If she is not given Cinderella, she can't get any other role. She'll take all the attention with her voice – which we don't want. Cinderella has to be the focus. Cinderella *has* to be the best performer, with the purest voice." Mrs. Murray explained sadly.

"That's it then," Bella gleefully agreed, trying unsuccessfully to hide her joy. "We can't have her."

"How can we reject her?" Janath sighed. "It feels so unfair to her talent."

"Let me do it," Bella willingly took the responsibility. She'll put this girl in her place.

There was a hush in the audience as Heather finished her performance.

It's so quiet! Did I mess up? Heather wondered to herself.

Suddenly, Damien and Janath stood up and clapped. The entire audience followed, and she received a thunderous applause.

Heather felt very happy.

She was surely going to get it!

But Damien and Janath looked sad and troubled as they took their seats.

Mrs. Murray also had a sympathetic expression on her face.

Bella seemed to be the only one with a triumphant expression.

"Heather! Wow! What a wonderful job!" she drawled.

Some in the audience clapped and whistled in agreement.

"Thank you!" Heather muttered shyly. She wasn't used to getting compliments.

"But you know, unfortunately, we can't give you a part in the play," Bella spoke with false sympathy.

"What?" Heather wondered, as the entire hall grew quiet.

Everyone seemed as shocked as her.

"Darling, look at yourself! You're fat and ugly. You can't seriously think we'll give you Cinderella!? Or any part for that matter!"

Damien tried to stop Bella at this point, but she shrugged him off with a toss of her hair and continued.

"Theatre is all about your appearance love, remember that next time you humiliate yourself on stage like this!"

Heather felt hot tears spring up and roll down her cheeks. She couldn't say anything.

"Lose some weight and come back," Bella snickered as Janath

hurriedly motioned for Heather to go.

Heather wished the earth would swallow her up and she would just die.

She willed her legs to take her out of the auditorium. She could see the sympathetic stares of some people in the audience. Few girls whispered, "Serves you right... Cinderella," and laughed mockingly.

Heather reached the door and went out without looking back. "I'm never going to perform. Ever again," she silently vowed.

There was a small stream next to an old banyan tree close to Heather's school. Students were generally warned not to go there without supervision in case they slip and fall. This meant that under the curtain of hanging banyan roots, Heather was well hidden from the outside world. No one could find her.

She sat under the tree, sobbed and occasionally wailed as she heard Bella's comments on replay in her mind; each time the words pierced her heart as if with a knife.

"How can I keep going? How can I go back to school after this? Everyone's going to laugh at me for trying to be Cinderella when I look so ugly," she moaned.

"Courage is not about being fearless but choosing to do the right thing even when you're afraid," Mr. David's kind voice rang in her mind as she had a flash back of what happened with Pavani.

"I can't give up!" she tried to be strong and will herself out of her misery.

"You absolutely can't" – a male voice chuckled, startling

Heather. Through tear-blurred vision, she looked through the curtain of banyan roots swaying gently in the wind and saw the tall, lanky figure of a boy in Oceans International's uniform with a senior prefect's badge.

Unlike her previous school, Oceans had a strict policy on students' attire. They were all required to wear uniforms in a tidy manner. The girls' uniform was a dark grey skirt paired with a white shirt. Boys' uniform was a long dark grey trouser worn with a white shirt. The shirts must have the Oceans logo of an anchor in the middle of a sea, woven into it.

Yikes! Heather thought. *I'm in trouble! I'm caught out here without supervision! Argh! How much worse can this day get?*

"I can't stay here, right? I'm so sorry..." Heather wiped her tears away. As she tried to get back on her feet, she stumbled on a root. A hand came through the curtain of roots to steady her.

"Thank you," she muttered as she looked at the boy's figure. Without the tears, her eyes cleared up and he was no longer blurry.

She felt her heart suddenly skip a beat as she really saw the boy in front of her.

He was tall and lanky but that wasn't it, he was very good looking.

He wore thick, black-rimmed glasses that hid two very concerned, warm and expressive eyes that focused on her.

His face was chiselled, and his lips were moving. *Oh! He's asking a question!* Heather realized with a start.

"Sorry... what was that? I didn't hear you properly."

"Are you okay?" He repeated slowly. "I'd hate to see you've hurt yourself in anyway"

Heather couldn't believe what she heard. Why was someone

who looked like (the clothed version of) the Greek statue of David talking to her and actually showing concern for her? This made no sense!

"I'm okay... thanks" Heather replied. She was flustered and struggled to hide it.

"You can stand on your own then?"

"What? Yeah... of course. I think I just stepped on one of the roots and lost my balance," she explained.

"Great... Do you want me to help you through this leafy curtain – back to class where I think you're supposed to be right now?"

Oh yeah. I have to be in class... Heather sighed.

"Thanks, I can manage."

"Um... okay... good" the boy replied with an eyebrow raised as he pointedly looked down.

Following his gaze Heather realized to her embarrassment that she was holding on to his hand in a vice-like grip.

All this time, he was unable to free his hand!

"Oh my gosh! I'm so sorry! I didn't realize..." Heather stammered and let go of his hands as if it was red-hot iron.

The boy chuckled and gave her a lopsided grin, which made her heart skip a beat – again.

"It's fine – I figured. You've had a tough day... so I get it."

"How...?"

"I was there at the auditions... I saw what happened"

"Oh..." grimaced Heather. So, he saw her getting humiliated and probably came to laugh at her.

"... Anyway, I would have known you were having a bad day just by that wailing! You know you're not that far off from school?"

"Was I that loud?" Heather was shocked.

"Yup!" that grin again popped up.

"So now that you're here, go ahead... laugh at me," Heather said bitterly as she mentally prepared herself for whatever that was to come.

"Laugh at you?" the grin disappeared. His face turned thoughtful and his expressive eyes filled with concern again.

"Why would I laugh at you?"

"Isn't that why you came to find me? Laugh at Heather – the ugly, fat, loser... before taking her to a teacher to be punished for going down to the banyan tree unsupervised."

The boy sighed, took both of her hands gently and looked into her eyes. He spoke slowly as if speaking to a child, as if he wanted her to believe every word he said.

"Heather, you are NOT ugly. You're beautiful. You are NOT a loser! You have SO much potential! You were easily the best performer I saw onstage today and after Bella's horrible speech I searched for you... to tell you that! You maybe a little chubby but that's something you can go on a diet and change. Don't put yourself down so much. You're awesome! I mean it! But I might actually have to go to a teacher if you keep crying like this," he teased as Heather broke into a sob.

"Why are you so kind to me?" Heather asked through her tears.

"Because I admire you. The courage you had to step on stage and perform like that... it is something I struggle with. I'd like to be your friend if that's alright with you?" He smiled gently as he waited for an answer.

"*YOU* want to be friends? With *ME*?"

"Yeah… I'd be honoured"

Heather couldn't believe what she was hearing.

Could she really trust this demi-god-like person in front of her, who not only treated her with compassion, but also wanted to be friends with someone like her… would he really want to be friends with her?

"Are you sure?" she asked hesitantly

"One hundred percent! Come-on… don't you like me?" He asked with feigned horror.

"No!" she replied – maybe a little too strongly. It brought out that adorable lopsided grin from the boy.

"I mean… yes… let's be friends" Heather quickly spoke as her cheeks got warm.

"You look cute when you blush"

"I'm *NOT* blushing!"

"Yes, you are!!!"

"And I'm *not* CUTE."

"Says who?"

Heather sighed and rolled her eyes.

"Would you let me be the judge of whether you're cute or not?"

"Fine… whatever… I don't even know anything anymore!"

"You know me!" He grinned again.

"Actually, I don't," Heather retorted.

Looking hurt, the boy winced.

"Sorry… I mean… I honestly haven't seen you before… I don't talk to many people, so…"

"It's fine… I get it," he smiled gently.

"You're not mad at me?"

"Of course not. Heather, we're friends now. I don't get mad at my friends over silly things."

"Thank you!" Heather smiled in relief.

The school bell rang in the distance.

"Shall we head back?" he asked her with a grin.

She really liked his grin, Heather decided as she said "Yes."

He led her through the thick curtain of hanging roots. As she emerged from the shadow of the banyan tree, the noon sun was too bright for her eyes and she shaded them. She looked at the boy who led her carefully across the stream. She wanted to call out to thank him again. He brought her out of her shadowy world into this light... that's when she realized she didn't know his name!

"Hey!" she called out, and the boy turned around to see if she was okay.

Seeing that she was, he raised his eyebrows quizzically. "Yeah?"

"I just realized something."

"Heather, I'm trying to get you across the stream safely. You really want to talk about your realization while we're in the middle of jumping across stones?"

"Well... it's kind of important"

Sighing, he gave in.

"What is it?"

"I don't know your name!" she replied smiling shyly.

That earned her a grin.

"Well... that won't do! We have to fix that immediately!"

Heather nodded.

"My name is Nathan De Zilwa" the boy grinned as he turned back. "Like the prophet Nathan in the Bible, who helped King

David... do you know that story?"

Heather shook her head.

She has never read a Bible. Whatever she knew about Christianity was from little things Jackson and Himalie talked about when she was small and was tutored by them.

"Well... Nathan was a prophet who heard from God. He helped a king called David by telling him what he should and shouldn't do... when David made mistakes, it was Nathan who brought God's correction to him..."

"Wow... you're named after someone amazing!" Heather said wistfully. "I'm just Heather. Kids used to call me sheep food when I was small. I guess it's because I'm useless."

Nathan stopped so suddenly that Heather almost crashed into him.

He turned to face her, his face-hardened. "'Just' Heather? You're not 'just' heather or sheep food or whatever else anyone has called you! You're SPECIAL Heather. A princess of God! Think that way! Don't you ever let anyone make you believe you're useless! Do you hear me?"

Startled by this sudden change in Nathan's demeanour, Heather didn't argue. She nodded in agreement.

"Good. Now listen, like Nathan was to David, I'm Nathan to you okay? If anyone treats you bad, says anything mean... you come and tell me! I'll help you". His grip on her hand tightened.

"He's strong!" Heather thought. "I'm so glad he's here. If I am a princess, then definitely he is a prince" Heather thought and smiled. She allowed Nathan to lead her, one rock at a time.

CHAPTER SIX

NATHAN WAS GLAD HE followed Heather when she ran out of the auditorium.

When Heather stepped on stage, Nathan could see that she was nervous. She was visibly shaking. As a prefect, he was required to assist Ms. Murray to maintain order in the auditorium during the auditions. That was the only reason for him to be anywhere near a stage.

He knew about the cruelty of the stage. His sister took her life because of the cruelty of people who bullied her for a single mistake she made on stage.

When he was eight years old, he had started to learn what he considered as the art of playing the guitar. His dream was to perform on stage like his big sister – so when he saw how her college class mates, cast members and even cyber bullies hounded her, it scared him.

He shuddered at the memory of his sister, crying in the living room as she read messages and bulletin board posts on 'Six Degrees' (which was the "Facebook" of the time). That day, Mom and Dad went out for a dinner party and Nathan watched helplessly as Natalie took Mom's car keys and went out.

He strongly felt that he should not let his sister go. He cried. Begged. Threw a mini tantrum. Nothing worked. Natalie's eyes seemed to look past him – she looked dead even when she was living and breathing. It scared him. So when Natalie hugged him and told him she's just going to the shops and she'd be back soon, Nathan didn't want to let go. But she gently pushed him aside, told him that she loved him and asked him to be safe. Her last words to him was to take care of Mom and Dad, before she turned around and left him – as he later found out, forever.

Few hours of agony passed as Nathan waited for Natalie. Finally, he heard the sound of a car that pulled in to park outside. It was his parents.

When he told them what happened, they were furious with Natalie for leaving him alone and taking the car without permission.

They tried calling her mobile, but she wouldn't pick up. As the hours went on, the knot in Nathan's stomach tightened. His parents were visibly worried. That's when the sirens wailed, and the police came to give them the news: Natalie was in a car crash and died on impact. She crashed her car into a tree. There were no skid marks, or signs of the brakes being used. In fact, evidence suggested she sped up before impact– so they knew it was a deliberate act of her own free will.

Since then, Nathan knew the power that bullies had to kill a person inside, even before they physically died. He began to fear the stage and gave up on his dream to perform. He was disgusted by bullies and cruel people who treated others like trash and made it his mission to help as many people as he could so that they won't end up like his sister – dead inside, lifeless, and without hope.

So when Heather stepped on stage, Nathan admired her

courage but also worried for her. She looked like a fresh victim for the 'stage'. Nathan paid close attention to her, especially when she said surprisingly that she was auditioning for *Cinderella*. She was cute; chubby, but cute. Her hair needed some work and she didn't look like stage material, but in her own way, Nathan saw that she was beautiful. However, he knew that the panel wouldn't select her for the lead, even though he wished they would, to spare her pain.

When she performed, he was enthralled. There was clearly more to her than what met the eye. She was like a different person when she started acting and her voice when she sang... it was like a nightingale!

Then, when Bella got up and gave her little speech, Nathan felt white-hot rage coursing through his veins. No one deserved that kind of treatment; especially not a girl who performed so well. It was pure malice and jealousy in Bella. Nathan was disgusted with her and the rest of the panel, who didn't stand up for Heather. Not even the teacher! "Did my sister endure this?" He wondered. As Heather dashed out of the auditorium, on impulse Nathan followed. He knew he should ask Ms. Murray for permission since he was still on prefect duty, but something compelled him to follow Heather. He should not lose sight of her. Even as he followed her at a distance, he wondered how he should approach her. He saw her once or twice at school before, but she was always on her own, in her little bubble. He never saw her speak to anyone or hang out with friends. His heart went out to her.

She was a walking reminder to him of Natalie. "I must help her before it's too late" Nathan resolved. When Heather approached the stream, Nathan wanted to run and stop her from doing anything stupid. *She's going to drown herself!* his thoughts were in a frenzy.

That's when Janath found him. He was running around trying to find Nathan because Ms. Murray was searching for him.

"Am I in trouble?" Nathan asked, all the while thinking frantically, "I can't leave her and go now! What if she..."

Janath grabbed a hold of him and interrupted his thoughts.

"What's wrong with you man? Snap out of it! It's not like you to dash out during duty!"

Nathan shrugged coldly – he did not forget Janath's silence when Bella harassed Heather. He remembered a quote he saw somewhere by Edmund Burke: "The only thing necessary for the triumph of evil is for good men to do nothing".

"Geez... loosen up dude. You're always so aloof. At least thank me for finding you and giving you the message."

"Thanks," Nathan replied briskly, scanning the area for Heather. While they were talking, she had vanished. She couldn't have jumped into the stream because he didn't hear a splash. For the second time, his thoughts were interrupted as Janath dragged him towards the auditorium.

Sighing in resignation Nathan hurried along with Janath to the auditorium, apologized to Ms. Murray and asked for her permission to be relieved of duty.

Luckily, the auditions were almost over and not many students were left, so Ms. Murray released him.

Nathan hurried back to where he saw Heather last. She was nowhere in sight.

Oh, God! Where is she? Is she okay? Please let me find her!

A sudden breeze stirred, and a leaf fluttered by his cheek, before landing in the stream to be caught up by the clear running water. His eyes followed the leaf, to where it stopped, near a thick curtain of roots hanging from a big banyan tree on the other side of the shore and he wondered whether Heather could be there.

As he drew closer to the stream, he heard the sound of someone wailing. He took a careful step forward, balancing on the rocks scattered across the stream.

Hang on Heather. I'm coming! I won't let you feel alone. I'll support you no matter what.

As he inched closer, he could make out Heather's figure. She sat on the ground near the roots and was hunched over as she sobbed.

Nathan realized that she didn't notice him yet, so he waited for an opportune moment to jump in and talk to her.

Suddenly, Heather lifted her head and declared to the empty space, "I can't give up!"

Seeing his chance, Nathan jumped in and replied, "You absolutely can't!"

Heather looked visibly startled. As they kept talking, Nathan firmly decided – *I'm helping her whether she likes it or not. She doesn't have friends? Well, I'll be her friend. I'm not going to let her go down my sister's path. Heather will live.*

"Hi Nathan!" Bella sweetly smiled as one of the hottest guys in her grade walked past her.

As usual, he didn't pay her any attention. Bella sighed, turning back to arrange her locker. "I don't know what's wrong with that boy. So many guys want to ask me out, but *he* won't even say hi!"

Bella slammed the locker door and sighed again as the

thought crossed her mind "... and he's the one person you want to be noticed by."

"Hey!" she suddenly heard his voice in the distance.

"Could it be? Did he *finally* notice her?" Bella looked around to see where he was and was shocked to see him talking not to her, but to Heather – that ugly, fat, good-for-nothing girl who had the nerve to try out for *Cinderella*.

He couldn't say hi to me, but he's talking to her? Is he blind? she inched closer, hidden from view by the trophy cabinet.

"How's class?" Nathan asked Heather gently.

"It was good. Same actually. Would have been fun if you were there," Heather replied softly.

Argh! She's totally sucking up to him! watching them together irritated Bella.

Nathan grinned. Wait. He grins? Bella has never seen him smile, let alone grin. He's always aloof and stoic. Never cracking a smile – always reserved and serious.

She felt jealousy gripping her heart. She really didn't like Heather.

"Well... I'm here now aren't I? What do you want to do after school?"

After school! They're meeting after school? Bella was horrified. Since when did they start this relationship? How did it happen under her very nose without her noticing?

"Library as usual. If you don't mind going there again," Heather's voice brought Bella back to reality.

"You know I don't mind," Nathan smiled.

"I'm sorry I'm not the most exciting person around," Heather replied.

Damn right. At least you know that! Bella thought as she

snickered inside. *The library! How dull! This won't be hard to break off – at all!* Bella felt herself ease up a little.

"Heather! I told you not to say things like that! I prefer being with you even in a library... its more interesting for me than being anywhere else without you"

Nathan's reply shocked Bella.

She felt a muscle twitch in her face. Bella was furious. What hold did this witch have over Nathan? She *had* to be a witch! There was *NOTHING* attractive about her!

She saw Heather blush. She was clearly smitten by him. Well... who wouldn't be! Especially when such sweet words came out of a guy like Nathan.

"You're such a good friend Nathan. Thank you!" Heather replied so softly that Bella almost missed that.

Friend? So that's it! He's just being a friend to her! But "she" clearly liked him to blush so much! He probably felt sorry for her and became friends, Bella's thoughts ran quickly.

Nathan took Heather's books and they walked towards the door.

Am I going to let it go? Just like this? Bella wondered.

She's fat and ugly – there's no way Nathan would fall in love with her... I just need to up my game to get his attention, Bella thought as she dismissed Heather.

No... I won't do anything now. I'll just wait and see... Bella thought to herself as Nathan disappeared through the door.

"Is that all you're having?" Nathan looked shocked as Heather took out her lunch.

They were seated outside close to the banyan tree. It became their special spot for lunch since the first time they met. Nathan wouldn't let her go across the stream because it was against school rules, but they found a shaded spot close to the stream with a view of the banyan tree to relax and enjoy their lunch.

"What? It's filling!" Heather replied.

"It's milk! A small carton of milk! How can that be enough for you?" Nathan wouldn't let it go.

"It's enough, okay?" Heather snapped, wishing Nathan would stop pestering her about her food.

It was a year since they met and Heather's feelings for Nathan grew with each passing day. Nathan treated her as a friend and Heather was painfully aware that he would never find her attractive if she didn't lose some weight. So she started skipping food for breakfast and dinner and drank a single carton of milk for each meal. It was difficult at first but soon her body adjusted.

She lost about ten kilos, but she was starting to feel the side effects of her bad diet. She felt more tired and irritable than usual, which Nathan also picked up on; he didn't realize she was on a diet until a few days ago.

If he found out the extent of her diet, Heather knew she'd be in trouble. Nathan was very protective of her.

"Okay! Chill! You don't have to snap!"

"Sorry..." Heather mumbled.

"Are you at least eating enough for breakfast?" Nathan was concerned.

"Um... I guess..." Heather was a bad liar.

"You guess? Which means you're not!" Nathan glared. "Heather, are you eating properly?"

Heather didn't know how to answer without lying.

Nathan kept glaring. The silence was filled with tension until Heather gave in and spilled the truth. Nathan was horrified!

"How could you treat yourself so badly? You need proper nutrition Heather! You can't diet like this!"

"Then how do you expect me to lose weight?" Heather choked out, stifling a sob that rose up. She hated seeing Nathan so worked up.

"I don't! Oh... you mean you've been trying to lose weight thinking I wanted you to?"

Heather feebly nodded.

"You silly goose! I told you I think you're beautiful; chubby or not. If you're losing weight, don't do it for me, do it for yourself: to feel better, to be healthier and you know what? Do it in a healthy way!"

"How? I can't afford to go to a gym! You know how it is at home!"

"Eat healthy!"

"Healthy food is expensive Nathan. My dad can't afford it"

"Fine! At least let me bring you lunch then. You could also come over for dinner. My mom wouldn't mind."

"Are you sure?"

"Yeah! You're my best friend. She knows all about you!"

Heather's heart warmed up.

Nathan had that effect on her. He was like warm coffee that took the chill away from her bones.

"I don't know how..."

"Stop it! I don't need your profuse gratitude speech"

"Hey! That's..."

"Unfair?" Nathan grinned. He knew her too well. Heather

really was one of a kind. Honest, pretence free and interesting in her own way. He never regretted making the decision to be her friend.

"Would you stop doing that?"

"Doing what?"

"Finishing my sentences for me!" Heather pretended to be angry.

Nathan reached out and ruffled her hair – as if she was a little kid.

"How can I when I know it annoys you so much?" He teased.

"Meanie!"

"Heather..."

"Yeah?" Nathan sounded serious again

"Would you like me to run with you in the morning? We live close by so if we wake up early before school and go for a run, it'll help you lose weight – plus its free exercise!"

"You'd do that for me?"

"Absolutely! You know I'd do anything to see you happy!"

Nathan had no idea just how happy Heather felt when he spoke so sweetly. She felt blessed to know Nathan. Something good did come out of that painful day she reminisced, thinking back on the day she was humiliated on stage.

It didn't sting anymore because Nathan's presence took the pain away. He was her joy.

"Okay then, let's do it!"

"Deal!"

"Sealed!" They bumped their fists – their little way of agreeing on something.

"Now, finish that milk and eat this!" Nathan placed one of his tuna sandwiches on her side of the table.

"What would I do without you?" Heather thought as she gratefully picked up his sandwich. It was good.

Bella tried hard to get Nathan to talk to her. She bumped into him, asked stupid questions for homework she already knew the answer to... NOTHING worked.

As the year went on and graduation came close, Bella was frustrated. She wanted him to be her partner for the graduation dance but at the rate things were going, it might as well be Heather.

Bella cringed at the thought of ugly, fat Heather taking Bella's rightful place in Nathan's life.

She's not fat anymore and if you think about it... she's actually not ugly, a voice inside her whispered. That didn't help Bella's rage. In fact, it intensified. *I've waited long enough. I can't wait anymore. It's war! Heather will be sorry for messing with me!*

"What?! You got into Penn State?" Heather couldn't believe what she was hearing.

"Yeah! College starts pretty much a week after graduation, so I'd have to leave the next day!" Nathan replied hesitantly.

He was excited he got into one of his top three picks for universities, but his heart was heavy with sadness at the thought of leaving Heather behind. "So soon? We have just... three weeks left!" Heather's excitement died down as the weight of this new reality hit her hard. She had gotten used to Nathan's support and constant company. She relied so much on him. It was difficult to think of facing high school without him.

"Yeah... three weeks..." Nathan mumbled. Penn State was so far from Colombo, thousands of miles away, across countries. There was no way they could see each other. This was something Heather tried not to think about when Nathan announced the top three universities that he was hoping to get into, out of the five he applied for. They were all far away.

"I'll miss you... so much" Heather mumbled back, as a single lonely tear rolled down her cheek, lonely as she felt at that moment.

"Hey now, don't cry" Nathan spoke softly. He leaned forward to wipe away the tears. "We can still keep in touch you know! We're not in the Stone Age! There's email, Facebook, Skype! We could talk and even see each other!" he smiled shakily as if trying to convince himself of what he was saying.

"It won't be the same..." Heather whispered.

"How so?" Nathan stubbornly pressed on.

"You won't be able to do this," Heather gestured at Nathan's hand, which was busily wiping each tear as they stumbled down.

Nathan grinned for a brief moment. "Fair enough..." he whispered and leaned back on his chair. They were in their usual corner table at the library. It was far from the librarian and far enough from the front that usually their surrounding was empty enough for them to talk and get away with it.

"You'll forget me when you go..."

"No, I won't!" Nathan's eyes flashed. He was irritated.

"How could you think that, after all we've been through this year?"

"I don't know... I'm just scared."

"Hey, listen! I'll visit you when I come home every semester break... okay? It's a promise!" He assured as he looked deep into her eyes.

Heather believed him. She trusted him. He had never broken a promise to her – ever.

"Besides, we have the internet! I'll bore you with my college tales every day on Skype... How's that?" Nathan tried to be cheerful.

Heather shook her head... "I don't have internet, remember? Can't afford it" she sighed heavily.

"Its fine. I'll wait for you to come home and meet me. A semester is what? Three months?"

"Yeah!" Nathan replied, feeling uneasy that he won't know how Heather would be doing for three whole months.

"I'll be fine." Heather tried to smile.

"You need to make new friends Heather. I don't want you to be alone after I go," Nathan insisted.

Sighing again, Heather replied, "I know... I know... I will! I promise!"

"I'm going to hold you to that!" Nathan grinned. "By the way, when we graduate, they usually have this graduation dance..." Nathan started, hesitating at first, wondering if Heather would agree to come with him. He knew how much Heather hated being in public places – let alone dance in one... but she was the only girl he was close to at school and really, the only person he'd share such an important day with.

"Yeah? I've heard some seniors talk about it." Heather interrupted. Suddenly, she was getting excited. She didn't dare hope Nathan would ask her for the dance when he could ask any girl in his grade. *Could he...? No! I shouldn't get ahead of myself,* Heather shook away the daring thought that crossed her mind suggesting that Nathan actually liked her as much as she liked him – more than as friends!

"So, we have to dance... you know... because it's a dance..."

"Yes Nathan, you usually dance at a dance," Heather tried to stifle a giggle. Nathan was clearly nervous. He stared as if to quiet her. "And you can't usually dance without a partner..." he continued.

"Do you..." Heather tried to help him along.

"Wait! Don't you dare interrupt me!"

She couldn't hold it any longer and burst out laughing!

He went beet red. It was the first time Heather saw him blush!

"Nathan, just say it!" She stopped laughing and spoke kindly, realizing this was difficult for him.

"Would you like to go for the dance with me?" Nathan blurted out, looking at her anxiously.

"Of course, Nathan! I'd be honoured" Heather graciously accepted.

"Phew! That was tough."

"I could see!" Heather giggled.

"The pain us men have to endure," Nathan grinned glancing at her comically.

"Oh shush! Drama queen!"

"Who, me?!" Nathan appeared shocked.

"Am I talking to anyone else?"

Nathan clutched at his heart, feigning hurt.

"Ouch! I think... someone just..."

Heather laughed loud, and Nathan joined in.

Three weeks like this. Only three weeks.

Heather wished time would stand still.

"What? You're saying NO? To *ME*?!" Bella shouted loud, refusing to believe what she heard.

She gathered up her strength and decided to ask Nathan for the dance since he didn't seem to have the courage to do it, but the nerve of the guy! When 'she' – Bella Van Asbeck, the queen of the drama club, the great, great granddaughter of a Dutch baron, stooped to ask him, a mere 'De Zilva', he had the nerve to say no!

He said no to *HER*!

Bella was outraged. Luckily, no one else witnessed her humiliation.

"Yes, Bella... thanks for asking but I've already given my word to go with someone else," he replied stoically before he walked away.

Bella stared at the back of the boy who rejected her and had the audacity to simply walk away. She seethed with rage. "It'd better not be Heather because if it is, I *WILL* destroy her... no... I will destroy them *both*!"

The wheels in her mind turned as she plotted her revenge plan. No one rejected her and got away with it unscathed – no one snubbed her like this and got away without pain – not even Nathan.

"Wow! You look beautiful," Nathan took in the vision before him. He was at her front porch to take her to the dance. Heather looked breath-taking with her hair styled and straightened, wearing a dreamy blue dress that highlighted her figure and brought out her complexion. "The weight loss did her good," Nathan thought, proud of his friend's transformation from the girl he met under the banyan tree to the breath-taking vision before him today.

"Thank you" Heather smiled shyly.

"How did you find that dress? Who styled your hair? Waiiiit... Heather, are you wearing make up?"

Heather laughed at Nathan's barrage of questions.

"My mom didn't take all of her things when she left, years back... I found this in her pile of clothes. Dad didn't have the heart to get rid of them. The hair and makeup is thanks to Himalie"

"Himalie...?"

"My neighbours! The shop owners across the street – remember I told you they tutored me? I'm pretty close with them."

"You mean Jackson and Himalie? Yeah! Of course I know them. Just didn't make that connection. I thought you made a new friend at school and didn't tell me," Nathan grinned feigning hurt.

Heather grinned back.

"You know pretty much everything to do with me Nathan... why would I hide it from you if I made a new friend?"

"I'm just messing with ya!" Nathan reached to ruffle her hair as if by habit, but Heather ducked in the nick of time.

"NO touching! You don't mess with the hair today!" she said firmly. Nathan realized too late that he would have messed up her carefully styled hair.

"Oops." He smiled sheepishly.

The clock chimed in her living room.

"Its six o'clock... shall we head off?" Heather asked.

"Yeah sure. Ma'am may I lead you to the dance?" Nathan comically offered his hand.

Laughing at his silliness Heather accepted it and they slowly made their way to the school auditorium.

The hall was decorated beautifully with fairy lights and it felt like she was entering into another world! She got the opportunity to experience this only because of Nathan. Heather looked up at the handsome boy beside her and found it hard to believe that she was his choice for this night. How drastically he changed her life since that day under the banyan tree. She only had gratitude and love towards him.

"Are you ready?" Nathan looked at her and she blushed, embarrassed to be caught staring at him.

"Yeah..." She mumbled.

"Thank you for coming with me. I know how much you hate being in the spotlight... in public places... and when we dance, you'll definitely catch people's attention... If you want to leave at any time, let me know okay? I won't force you to stay long."

"Nathan, you're leaving tomorrow! This is the last few hours we get to spend with each other. I want you to enjoy it. I want it to be a good memory for you before you head off to Penn State."

Nathan squeezed her hand gently.

"Thank you!"

"It's the least I could do for all you've done for me," Heather smiled.

They stepped inside and mingled amidst the hundreds of students who'd come to enjoy the night. The music blared from the speakers, inviting them to the dance floor and there were few teachers to maintain discipline. They were all dressed up and looked different. Everyone looks great, Heather thought, suddenly conscious of her appearance.

Nathan felt Heather tense up beside him. She looked around and seemed to take everything in. Was she uncomfortable? No... That was not it. He noticed that she fiddled with her hair and dress. He knew she did that when she was conscious of her appearance. Nathan chuckled inside. She really had nothing to worry. She outshone every other girl here that night – at least in his eyes.

"Hey! Heather!" Nathan leaned in and whispered.

"Yeah...?" She fidgeted.

"You look gorgeous!"

Heather stopped and looked up at him – warming his heart with a radiant smile.

"Thank you! That's the first time you said that."

"That you're gorgeous?"

"Yeah! It's usually – you're cute or you're beautiful..."

"Well... aren't they the same? I'm appreciating your beauty!" Nathan shrugged.

"Yeah... but when you said gorgeous, it felt different."

"Well you *do* look different. It's the first time you're dressed up like this..." Nathan held her gaze and smiled softly, "You really look great Heather."

Hearing that from Nathan was enough for Heather. She stopped comparing herself and feeling conscious. She was going to help him enjoy the night.

They approached the dance floor and soon they were lost among the crowd. The song shifted, and Heather heard *"Don't stop believing... Hold on to the feeling..."* blaring through the speakers. Heather smiled to herself, agreeing with the band 'Journey'; *I'm definitely going to hold on to this feeling – it will be a good night.*

"Oops! I'm sorry!" a boy crashed into Heather and spilled juice all over her dress. He was tall – like Nathan and his longish hair cascaded into his face like a waterfall before he brushed it aside to see Heather better. He wore a serious, worried expression clouding what seemed to be an otherwise carefree, boyish face. Heather thought he looked like a nice guy but felt Nathan tense up next to her. "It's okay... I can wash it up," she smiled. The boy smiled gratefully and offered his hand to her. "I'm Mikesh Rajeshvaran. Nice to meet you!" Before she could shake his hand, Nathan pinned him to the nearby wall. "I don't think you're actually sorry... You don't crash into a girl, spill your drink all over her and then try to charm your way out of it, if you're actually sorry".

"Whoa! Chill old boy! I'm not trying to 'charm' your girl here".

"Nathan, it's okay... really... I'm fine," Heather gently grabbed his free hand.

Nathan felt the built-up, white-hot rage fade out...a little.

"You're not supposed to be here, Mikesh."

"Neither is she!"

"She's my partner!" Nathan's hands curled up in a fist.

Heather sensed that Mikesh and Nathan had some history between them and were not in good terms.

"Well... I'm also invited by someone!"

"Who?"

"That's none of your business!"

"I'm a prefect! It is my business!"

"It's the graduation ball dude. You don't have any authority here after tonight. Would you chill?"

Heather gripped Nathan's hand, hard, and while dragging Nathan away from Mikesh spoke aloud, "I think this will stain if I don't wash it now... Nice meeting you Mikesh!" Nathan tried to struggle a little and Heather whispered strongly "Let's GO!" and turned towards the washrooms.

"Nice meeting you too, babe! I'll see you around," Mikesh grinned as they left.

Nathan was not pleased. He was not happy about the way he lost his temper in front of Heather and he was not happy that Mikesh of all people noticed Heather at a time when he wouldn't be around to protect her from his 'influence'. Mikesh was bad news – a good for nothing loafer. They were classmates once, but he kept flunking and couldn't pass on to the next grade because of his lifestyle. He took school as a joke and skipped class countless times to go smoke up outside. Nathan had caught him and initially had let him off with stern warnings because he felt sorry for him, but realizing Mikesh was not changing his behaviour, Nathan had no choice but to dutifully report him to the teachers each time he was caught cutting class or smoking up. Mikesh hated him for it. Mikesh believed that "rules were meant to be broken" and that Nathan was a wet blanket who seemed to be on his case. Mikesh saw Nathan to be just like Mikesh's father – controlling, sticking to rules, no fun – and he hated Nathan for it.

Nathan disliked Mikesh for wasting his potential. He remembered how smart and talented Mikesh used to be when they were together in middle school. It was once he joined Oceans International through a scholarship that he started rebelling, skipping class and wasting time. Nathan hated the irresponsible way Mikesh wasted the contributions that funded his scholarship. When Mikesh sneered at him and tried to make things difficult as he carried out his prefect duties, Nathan would sometimes wonder whether Mikesh was just jealous of him for some reason, because he had observed that Mikesh never bothered to pick fights with other prefects who caught him and reported him for detention.

"What are you doing here? Alone?" an annoying voice Nathan knew, sadly too well, snapped him out of his unpleasant thoughts to an equally unpleasant reality.

"Bella!" He knew it. She needed to go before Heather came out of the washroom. Nathan did not want Bella to treat Heather any worse than she already had.

"You didn't answer my question…"

Nathan hesitated.

"Oh please! Save it. You're obviously waiting for your precious Heather"

"If you knew that, why did you bother asking?"

"I wanted to make sure. She looked so different."

"Jealous again?"

"Hardly. I actually feel sorry for her," Bella gave an unpleasant expression that chilled him to the bone.

"What do you mean?"

"Nothing."

"Spill it." Nathan knew she was hiding something – something important that he had to know.

"You're such a bad, bad boy Nathan"

"What?" He was confused.

"You seem so good. Smart. Never doing anything out of line... but you're truly such a bad person"

"Are you still on my case because I said no to you?" Nathan retorted

Bella's eyes flashed with anger.

He had hit a sore spot.

"I don't care about you so much that it mattered to me Nathan. I have a date. I don't have to go begging."

"Then, what's your point?"

"You really don't see how you're hurting Heather, do you?"

"I'm hurting Heather?" that was the last thing Nathan expected to hear from Bella. Truly confused, Nathan asked, "How?"

"You're leading her on! She's clearly in love with you and you are making her believe that you love her too... just to get all her attention and maybe even to have her as a date for tonight!" Bella spoke in a matter of fact way.

"Are you mad? Heather doesn't think of me that way! We're friends! I never led her on!"

"Why do you think she lost all that weight *after* you became friends with her?"

"Because she wanted to be healthy!" Nathan remembered

something the moment those words were out of his lips.

Really? Is that honestly what you believe?

Nathan started to remember Heather telling him that she wanted to lose weight because she thought he wanted her to. He brushed it off at the time and didn't pay too much attention to it because he was more concerned with her poor nutrition.

"You're just afraid because Heather looks great now, that she'll take your place in the drama club," Nathan didn't want Bella to see that she got him.

"Huh? I'm leaving this place now Nathan! It doesn't matter anymore. Just like how it won't matter to you to leave behind a girl with a broken heart."

"We're just friends!"

"That's what YOU think! I feel so sorry for that girl for being in love with an oaf who don't even notice her feelings!"

"STOP IT!"

"It's true! You speak so sweetly to her, your words dripping with honey...she blushes... totally swooning over it and all along, you're only playing with her heart without even realizing it! Such a bad boy!"

"You're wrong!" Nathan whispered. Doubt filling up his eyes.

Bella knew she got him.

"Am I?" she scornfully replied.

Nathan remembered the many times Heather blushed when he teased her for fun. He felt dread enter his heart and a heavy weight. He was feeling guilty!

Get a grip Nathan! This makes no sense! Why are you feeling guilty? You didn't know! he tried to calm himself down. Bella wouldn't let go.

"Don't even try to excuse yourself thinking you didn't know

Nathan. You knew! Deep inside. She's so stupidly transparent... anyone watching the two of you knew she liked you. You knew it too, but you were so selfish, you ignored it. You saw the signs, but you were so stuck being a superhero to her, basking in her admiration and attention, you didn't want to address reality. You're a jerk Nathan – a bigger jerk than I've ever been to her! You've cornered her into a place where she can't escape. You're her world now! She'll be so broken when she realizes the truth!"

Nathan realized with horror what Bella was about to do. She was going to tell Heather about this!

Guilt tore at his heart. All he wanted to do was to help Heather, but it looked like he was just hurting her all along.

Just then, Heather came out – her dress cleaned up, beaming with joy.

"It's gone Nathan! I managed to take it all off!" she smiled radiantly.

How could he face her? How could he? Knowing now that he would never be able to be normal without worrying about whether he's leading her on or not? How was Heather ever going to forgive him when she finds out what a blind idiot he's been?

"Nathan...? OH!" Heather finally noticed Bella.

"Hi, Heather!" Bella sweetly spoke, her words dripping with malice.

"Hi..." Heather replied to Bella, her eyes still fixed on Nathan.

"What's going on?" Heather wondered. Nathan looked pale – like he just got bad news. *Bella is here... this can't be good.*

"I was just having a small chat with Nathan here," she innocently spoke while fluttering her long eyelashes.

"Okay..."

"Aren't you going to ask what it's about?" Bella fluttered her eyelashes again.

Heather found it distracting. "It's between you and Nathan. I don't need to know," She grabbed Nathan's hands to get him to go. They were cold and sweaty. This is not normal. He looked... afraid?

"I think you do need to know Heather about your 'friend' here! Or... maybe it's Nathan who needs to know about you and the secret you've been hiding!"

Nathan came back to focus.

"Secret? Heather hides nothing from me!"

Heather blushed as she heard the conviction Nathan had of her. She blushed knowing that Bella has stumbled upon a landmine. She did have a secret from Nathan – a tiny secret... a secret that could change their friendship forever... that she liked him, more than as a friend.

"Oh, but she does have a secret from you!" Bella pressed on. "Tell him Heather! Tell him why you lost all that weight! Tell him why he makes your heart flutter... Tell him how much you looooooove him," malice just poured out of Bella's words.

Heather was frozen. "How could she tell him? He's going to hate her for daring to fall in love with him when she wasn't even worth him. He won't ever want to be friends with her again. She's going to lose him."

Nathan looked shaken. He turned to her, his eyes looking pained, like he was suffering inside. "Tell me she's lying, Heather."

Heather felt like a knife was thrust into her heart. *He didn't want her to like him! Her feelings were a burden to him. That's why he looked like he's in pain! Bella must have already told him!*

"I... I..." Heather stammered, unable to get the words out.

"It's okay... It's me! You can tell me anything," Nathan gently spoke.

"I'm sorry Nathan... she's telling the truth!"

Nathan looked like she slapped him across the face.

He took a step back, his face becoming even more pale. *He really didn't want her to like him. It's just as she feared! He hates her now, just like her mom. She never deserved to be by his side!*

"I... I think I'm going to go now," Heather stifled a sob. She didn't want to him to see her cry and ruin the night even more for him. "Bye, Nathan." Heather turned to go.

Quick as lightening, Nathan grabbed her hand. His face was twisted with sorrow and pain. He looked like he aged within minutes. He looked deep into her eyes and said three words that made her feel like the knife that pierced her heart was taken out, only to be replaced by three more – the pain was unbearable.

He said, "I'm sorry Heather," with the finality of a goodbye.

She shrugged his hand off and ran into the night, as the tears streamed down her face.

She was never going to see him again.

CHAPTER SEVEN

I̶T WAS TIME FOR NATHAN to leave home. He took one last look at their dining table. Memories flooded his mind. Just a few days ago, Heather was here. They ate steak for dinner and Mom cracked a joke that cracked them up until he almost choked. It felt empty now. His life felt empty and his heart felt cold. The way Heather looked at him when she said bye... and even when he apologized, it was full of hurt. He saw that her eyes were full of unshed tears. He knew when she left him, she'd be crying, and it pained him to know that this time, he was the cause of her tears.

"Aren't you going to see Heather?" Mom walked in with her handbag and car keys in hand. She was supposed to drive him to the airport. Dad was unable to see him off because of a meeting at work but that was okay. He understood his father's schedule.

Nathan shook his head, sighing as he wondered again if he was doing the right thing by leaving without seeing her again. Bella's words repeated in his mind.

I don't want to give her the wrong impression and lead her on even more and hurt her more in the process, he reasoned why he shouldn't see her.

"I don't think she'd want to see me, Mom".

"Why? What happened?"

"Long story. I think I've been a jerk and hurt her really bad."

"Did you say sorry?"

"Yeah…"

"And…?"

"I don't think she forgave me, Mom. She looked really hurt and she ran away from the dance."

"Oh dear…" Mom sighed.

She really liked Heather and enjoyed having her around. "Maybe she just needs more time".

Nathan sighed. He wished that were the case. He wished they would be friends again. He'd hate it if he had unknowingly ruined their friendship by his blindness to her feelings. He couldn't believe that out of all people, *he* was the inconsiderate jerk to Heather.

"Look… Nathan, you need to leave this behind. You're starting college. It's a new chapter in your life and you need to focus on your education. Penn State isn't cheap!"

"I know, Mom… I'm just going to miss her… I hate leaving when things are like this."

"Why don't you talk to her when you're back for break? That'll give her enough time."

"Yeah… I guess…" Nathan sighed as he picked up his bags. The luggage was heavy but not as heavy as his heart. Nathan moved to leave the house. Turning back one last time to glance at the dining room, Nathan heard the twinkle of Heather's laughter and remembered her sitting at her chair. "I'll come back for you Heather. We'll make things right. I promise!"

School lost all its colour and meaning to Heather. She went dutifully but the laughter, fun and light she enjoyed during last year was gone, vanished with Nathan's departure from her life. She felt empty and listless. *He didn't come to say goodbye. He really must hate me now like Mom did...* Heather often wondered. *I guess he couldn't wait to go... just like Mom*, she'd think before breaking into a sob. *Why do people I love hate me so much? What's wrong with me? Why me? What wrong did I do to anyone?* Self-pity often overwhelmed her. Crying was her new norm.

It was close upon a month since Nathan left and each night, Heather's tears soaked her pillow. She missed him. She hated that he won't be back for her... He was not going to keep his promise to come back. Guilt and condemnation ate her up as she lamented her feelings for him. "I wish I didn't like him this much! If I didn't, we'd still be friends and I'd be able to look forward to meeting him during his break!"

As it is, life felt dreary to Heather. There was nothing to look forward to. The light, meaning and joy of living that she felt when Nathan was around was gone. She was back to her old routine. Her dad came home at night as usual and hardly spoke to her, as was his norm. She was invisible at school again... well, except to Mikesh.

Mikesh kept trying to be Heather's friend. He invited her for house parties and so on... but Heather remembered how Nathan didn't seem to like him and felt uneasy about accepting Mikesh's invitations. In fact, there was a party happening that night and Heather was wondering whether to go.

Her father wouldn't care. He wouldn't even notice if she was at home or not. Nathan... well, Nathan clearly didn't care either.

He left without saying goodbye and he was never coming back into her life. His apology made that clear. *So... why aren't you going for the party then?* a voice whispered in her mind. *Why aren't I?*

Suddenly Heather couldn't find any excuses. She was sick of moping around in self-pity and feeling sad without Nathan. She wanted some control back in her life. She wanted to find something to be happy about. She wanted to go and have fun without Nathan – or try to, at least. *Yes, that's it. You know what, I'm going to go and enjoy myself,* Heather decided.

Mikesh was surprised to see Heather at Dasun's party. He was about ready to give up on her and Bella's plan, but it all changed when she willingly came to the party. He couldn't believe she withstood his charms for a month! He was very annoyed it took this long to break her free from Nathan's hold over her life.

That's what he hated about 'goody two shoes' controlling people. They manipulated people to do what *they* wanted. They gave no chance for people to be themselves and make their own choices. They judged you if you didn't act the way *they* thought was right; Nathan was a carbon copy of Mikesh's dad.

The bitterness stirred within him. "Oh no! I'm not going to let you ruin my life!" He exclaimed as he took a sip from his glass. The alcohol felt good as Mikesh felt it rushing down his throat. He felt the warmth burst through his body. "Booze – the cure for all things," Mikesh chuckled bitterly as he looked at his glass filled with the poison that he knew would someday be the death of him if he continued to live the way he did. He wasn't stupid. He knew he wasn't going anywhere the way he led his life, but a part of him has given up on living a normal life the way his dad wanted him to. He wanted to be different – to follow his own path. So, every time his heart felt even the smallest bit of pain, he turned to a trustworthy glass of vodka that faithfully soothed him. "Time to give you some freedom, Heather," Mikesh snickered as he grabbed another glass of vodka from the counter where Allie – Dasun's girlfriend had already passed out.

The small, crowded, dimly lit house was filled with a curtain of smoke. Heather's vision was hazy, and her eyes stung. The stench of alcohol rose up and made Heather gag. Music blared from speakers set up somewhere and people were dancing, drinking and smoking all around her. None of them seem to mind the smoke or the stench. She had never seen something like this before. She felt like she had entered a completely different world.

Mikesh walked up to her with a grin on his face. Heather noticed that his grin was nothing compared to Nathan's. She couldn't help comparing them.

"Hey! You made it!" He shouted to be heard over the loud din of music.

"Yeah... I don't think I should stay long though... I should probably go," Heather felt uneasy. She felt her head throb. The smoke, stench and loud music gave her a headache.

"Come on... stay a bit... live a little! It'll be fun!"

"Fun? Really?"

"Yeah..." Mikesh rolled his eyes. "Why else do people come for parties, stupid? If it wasn't to have fun?"

"I dunno... I just don't feel..."

"Relaxed? Here, have some! It'll help!" Mikesh handed her one of the glasses he brought with him.

It looked like water and Heather was grateful as she suddenly realized how parched she was.

She gulped it all down but realized it wasn't water as the liquid made her throat feel like it was on fire. She almost choked.

"Was that...?"

"Alcohol? Yeah..." Mikesh chuckled as he ran his hand over the long silky strands of his hair. "I didn't think you'd chug it all."

"I thought it was water!" Heather found herself giggling. She felt lighter and more relaxed.

Mikesh laughed and smiled.

"Shall I get you another?"

Alcohol really didn't feel so bad, Heather thought wondering why she'd always had such a negative idea of it. "Yes please," she heard herself say.

Mikesh grinned mischievously and took her hand.

"Come with me... Allie over there brought some vodka but she was gone when I checked on her a few minutes back. She couldn't even finish the bottle. We'll dig into it and help her out!"

"Allie?"

"Dasun's girlfriend. Dasun's the guy who lives here," Mikesh explained, pointing out a bearded guy with tattoos on his muscled arms. He was smoking with some men in a corner and paid no attention to them.

"He doesn't look our age!"

"That's because he's not"

"How do you know him?"

"I know many people, Heather," Mikesh replied mysteriously while he poured her a glass and turned to fill his own.

"Okay..." Heather said out loud, glancing at Allie who seemed asleep at a party with such loud music. Heather was concerned for her. "Is she okay?"

"She's just passed out."

"Passed out? What do you mean?"

"That's what happens if you drink too much of this stuff," Mikesh pointed at the glass in her hand. Seeing her look of panic, Mikesh hurriedly reassured her. "Don't worry, it won't happen if you only drink a few glasses...Allie probably emptied an entire bottle before she started on this one."

True to his words, Heather saw an empty bottle of vodka lying next to Allie on the floor. "Come-on Heather! Don't worry! I'll take care of you!" Mikesh reached to adjust a strand of loose hair that had settled on her cheek. She let him and relaxed, taking another sip from her glass. It did make her feel good. "Good girl!" Mikesh grinned and he took out his phone. It was a Nokia – N95!

Heather gasped "Isn't that the latest Nokia?"

"Yup!" Mikesh grinned proudly.

"I've never seen one! I heard its expensive!"

Mikesh roared with laughter.

"I'll let you check it out... but first, let's take a photo! Hold out your glass!"

"But why? I don't think it'll be good if people at school find out we've been drinking!"

"You really think I'll share this anywhere? It's just for me! I love capturing important moments!" Mikesh grinned.

"Important moments?" Heather wasn't sure what he meant.

"Heather's first experience of vodka with me!"

"Oh...! Okay..." Heather relaxed.

Mikesh came close and wrapped an arm around her. She felt a little uncomfortable, but she couldn't move. His grip was strong.

"Where's your glass?"

"Here!"

"Okay... Raise it up!"

Heather obeyed.

"Good girl, now... smile!" he said as he held out his phone and took a photo with her.

"Okay great!" Mikesh smiled looking at the photo he took. "Now... let's hit the dance floor!" He got her to finish her second glass of vodka and dragged her to the throng of moving bodies.

He's not like Nathan, Heather couldn't block the thought that came. *Nathan never dragged me around.*

Heather firmly kicked that thought out of her mind. She didn't want to think about Nathan – not when she was finally feeling alive without him. The alcohol really helped. She allowed Mikesh to lead her in the dance floor and he was good to her. The only annoying thing was, he had a habit of taking out his phone and taking photos with her every now and then, in different poses while dancing. Heather was in a generous mood by the time she had a third glass of vodka, so she didn't mind it too much.

"Do you want to try something?" Mikesh asked her when they took a break from dancing.

"What?"

Mikesh pulled out a cigarette and lit it. He seemed to take it in slowly and exhaled a white puff of smoke into the air.

Heather was shocked. Would she really dare try this?

So far, Mikesh helped her have fun, trying once won't hurt her – would it?

"Just try it..." Mikesh took it out of his mouth and gave it to her.

"How?"

"Just keep it in your mouth like this..." Mikesh explained after placing the cigarette on her lips.

Smoking was not fun. Heather decided as she coughed after her first try. Mikesh laughed and took the cigarette from her but not before taking a photo of her trying to smoke.

"I guess that's not for you then," he chuckled.

"Yeah... DEFINITELY not! I think I'll stick to vodka," Heather replied.

"Want one more?"

"I dunno... I feel so light already... Maybe I shouldn't."

"Okay... last glass?"

Heather gave in. "Last glass for real... okay?"

It was such a different night full of new experiences for her. "I guess this is another way of having fun," Heather thought as she lost herself in one more glass of vodka.

Mikesh knew when Heather was almost gone. When he watched her try everything he placed before her, like an innocent little child, he felt sorry for her. She was a good kid. *I'm sorry I have to do this to you but it's for your own good you know...* Mikesh thought as he mentally went through Bella's plan. He really had nothing against Heather, but he hated how she was so controlled by Nathan. If Mikesh could give her a taste of freedom even if it meant hurting her a little – it was worth it; he justified. *Of course, it's killing two birds with one stone because I get to wipe that arrogant smirk off Nathan,* Mikesh stiffened at the memory of Nathan pinning him to the wall at the dance. He was just following Bella's instructions when he spilled his drink over Heather, but he genuinely wanted to know her when she responded kindly, even after he ruined her dress. Any other girl would have bitten his head off. Nathan however got in the way; he was such a control freak. So, when Bella revealed the rest of her plan, Mikesh agreed, just to get back to Nathan and also, as he later justified, for Heather's freedom.

Heather drunkenly suggested they dance some more and almost tripped on Mikesh, interrupting his thoughts. Luckily, he caught her. He knew it was time to take her home. She found her balance as she leaned against him and she snuggled close to him as he put his arm around her to steady her.

Mikesh led her to her house and took one last photo.

"Hey... we're here," he whispered, not wanting her to get into trouble.

Heather smiled at him sweetly "We're home?"

"Yeah..." he felt himself smile back.

She really was one of a kind. I guess he understood why Nathan was protective about her – Mikesh grudgingly found himself agreeing with Nathan for the first time.

"Okay then... thank you for tonight Mikesh. Bah-bye" Heather unsteadily waved and went inside the house.

Mikesh waited for her to go in and slowly made his way home. He took his phone out and went through the photos he took that night and sighed as he thought about what he was about to do. *I'm sorry Heather... but it really is for your own good.*

Nathan looked at the calendar on his table. It was covered with sticky notes that reminded him of assignments due before the upcoming final examination week. He was in his dorm room at Penn State. It was a studio room and he loved its small, cosy atmosphere. It couldn't replace his room at home of course, but it was comfortable enough for his time at the college.

Nathan couldn't believe how fast time flew. It's already six months since he left home and came to Penn State. He was busy getting used to life as a college student, working part time at the college dining hall while managing his class work. He barely had time to sleep, let alone call home or use the Internet. Things were more challenging than he thought it would be. It was definitely more work than in high school. Nathan remembered some images he saw on Facebook a few months back and frowned. Mikesh had tagged him in a post with some photos of Heather. Heather was not alone; she was with Mikesh in every single photo. She was drinking and smoking in the photos – they were things Heather didn't do when she was with him. What got her to change? Nathan was worried for her at first but then, unpleasant thoughts began to bombard him.

Why was she with Mikesh? Doesn't she know what kind of person he was? Did she already replace him with Mikesh? The poisonous green serpent called envy gripped his heart. He hoped Heather was okay and felt guilty for what happened with her, but jealousy got the better of him. *How could she hangout with Mikesh? So soon after he left! How could she change like that? Wasn't their friendship special to her like it was to him? Was she faking it with him?* He felt like she had replaced him completely with Mikesh. *That's probably why she never contacted him after he left*, he remembered thinking bitterly. *Well if she was going to forget him so quickly, he'd give her a taste of some of her own medicine,* he thought before scrolling on Facebook and finding one of his old friends who was also studying with him at Penn State.

Evelyn was one of his earliest friends in high school. She was pretty, elegant, efficient, hardworking and was also nominated to be a prefect at the same time as he was. She always knew just the right thing to say and was quite an inspiration to him. Initially, they hit it off quite well, talking and sharing things a lot. However, when it was time for final prefect selections, Evelyn became too competitive. She stopped talking to him and disappeared for a while to suck up to the seniors. Then, when both of them were prefects, she became close to him again. Soon however, she started liking a senior and wanted him to notice her. She tried everything in the books and Nathan supported her efforts, but when it seemed like having Nathan around was an inconvenience to their budding romance, she dropped him again like he was a hot potato that was scalding her precious, perfectly manicured hands. Nathan hated her disloyalty and flakiness. He did not try to be friends with her again, even when she tried to reconnect after her relationship with the senior did not seem to work out. Instead, when Nathan met Heather, he was happily preoccupied with their friendship.

Heather was so much better as a friend, he remembered thinking and sighed even as he looked at Evelyn's profile picture. Evelyn was dressed in a green dress and looked great as she always did. Knowing the coldness of her heart that can easily use and reject him without the blink of an eye, Nathan hesitated before clicking the message option. Mikesh's pictures with Heather flashed in his mind's eye. Blinded by envy and rage, Nathan did it. He sent a message to Evelyn and thus, their friendship was rekindled. However, it only took few weeks for Nathan to realize Evelyn could never replace Heather.

The conversations that used to be lively and engaging with Evelyn in the past, now felt forced and dull. He sent funny emoticons and it looked on the surface like they were having a fun time if anyone was to check their message history, but his heart felt empty and dead. It wasn't real. Their friendship felt fake after the genuine friendship he experienced with Heather. There was a difference in the quality of their relationship. As silly, awkward, insecure and imperfect as Heather was at times, Nathan loved her loyalty, love and the genuineness about her – a quality that Evelyn could never bring into their friendship. Even if Heather found a replacement for him in Mikesh, it was too late when he realized that he couldn't find a replacement for her in Evelyn – or in anyone else.

Nathan sensed it was too late because he broke the promise he made to Heather. Rather than coming back home to visit her during his first break (like he promised), he chose to stay at Penn State to rekindle his friendship with Evelyn. Since the break was too short and flights were too expensive for him to leave college for home and come back, he justified that it wasn't financially worth it to make the trip home for just two weeks. His mom advised him to stay as well, so he agreed, telling his mom to check on Heather for him. However, truth was, his heart's motive was not pure. It was motivated with the jealous anger he felt at being replaced by Mikesh.

Looking at the calendar again, Nathan realized how much time has passed. He regretted not going back home for that first break. He didn't hear back from his mom about Heather. Remembering the photos grimly, Nathan wondered for the umpteenth time whether he should have gone home without getting caught up in his jealousy and fruitlessly trying to replace Heather with Evelyn.

Nathan's eyes landed on his mobile phone sitting idly on his table top.

He has not heard back from his parents in a long while, so he decided to call them. He'll be home in two weeks and he missed them. His mom picked the phone.

"Is that Nathan?" her voice sounded strained.

"Hi Mom! How are you?"

"Good! How are you? How's everything going?"

"Good... I'm sorry I didn't call you in weeks. Had so much work..."

"It's fine darling, I understand. I'm glad you're focusing on your studies," She sounded different.

Nathan sensed that something was wrong.

"Mom... what's wrong?"

"Nothing!"

"Mom..."

"Just come home Nathan. Don't worry. We're fine"

The phone clicked and went dead.

Did Mom just hang up on me? Nathan was surprised. Something clearly wasn't right, and he knew her well enough to know that she didn't want him worried during his finals for the term. A familiar knot tightened in his stomach even as he thought, I guess I'll have to wait till I go home to find out.

"Finally! I'm home!" Nathan sighed as he spread himself out on his bed. It felt good to be back on his own bed. The dorm bed was fine but there was something special about your own bed at home.

Looking at a photo frame on his table, Nathan smiled. It was taken on Christmas when Heather came over to celebrate with them. Remembering that day Nathan chuckled. Heather was so excited because it was her first Christmas dinner. Her dad didn't believe in God and she had never been to church. She had so many questions.

Nathan's smile faded as he remembered the way his mom sounded on the phone two weeks back. He didn't see her yet because he took a taxi home. He wanted to surprise her and arrived a day early than he was supposed to.

He heard the door click shut downstairs and he could hear his mom's voice! It was so good to hear her so close. Nathan wanted to run and give her a big hug and see the surprise on her face.

He silently opened the door and tiptoed downstairs. He paused near the edge of the staircase as he heard another voice. It was the familiar voice of a lady; they've got visitors. "Great!" Nathan thought grinning in mischievous glee. "She's never going to expect me now!"

"Himalie, I don't know how I'm going to break this to Nathan," his mom's voice broke into a sob.

That got Nathan's attention. *What's going on?* he wondered. He stopped in his tracks and strained his ears to hear.

"They were such close friends..." he heard Himalie reply.

"After what happened to Natalie... do you remember her? My little girl?" Nathan's mom seemed to pause to get herself together as Himalie comforted her, "I don't know how he would take it if he finds out what happened to Heather..." his mom sobbed.

Nathan felt his legs weaken. *Natalie? Heather? Please don't tell me...*

"But she's still alive, isn't she?" Himalie's words interrupted his thoughts.

"Only by the grace of God! It was a miracle! She jumped from such a high bridge and the child couldn't even swim!"

Nathan felt blood rush into his head. He felt dizzy. He couldn't bear this any longer. He had to know.

"Mom?" Nathan croaked, managing to come downstairs.

There was silence for a moment, the shifting of chairs and the sound of feet rushing towards him.

It was Himalie.

"Oh dear! Nathan's here!"

"I wanted to surprise Mom..."

His mother appeared with eyes red from tears. "Oh... darling, I'm sorry... I didn't..."

"What happened to Heather, Mom? Is she...?" he couldn't bring himself to finish the sentence.

"Shall we all sit down before we continue with this conversation?" Himalie grabbed him by his arm and gently guided both him and his mother to the dining room table.

They sat and for a moment there was silence. Nathan's mother didn't seem to know how to respond.

"She's not dead love, if that's what you're worried about" Himalie finally spoke up frankly.

Nathan sighed with relief, suddenly feeling strength return.

"Then, what was this story about a bridge?"

His mom took his hands gently and spoke softly.

"She tried to jump off a bridge and she would have drowned, but God saved her darling."

"WHAT?!" Nathan shouted. "Why would she do that?"

"A lot seemed to have happened to her after you left" Himalie responded, "She was involved in some way with a boy named Mikesh...at least that's what I heard from the students who came to our store. They were gossiping about seeing her with that girl who was mean to her once, what's her name...."

"Can't be Bella?" Nathan tensed.

"Yes! That's right! Bella... she was with Bella a few weeks before the incident" Himalie remarked.

"Bella?" Nathan was confused. *What's she doing here? I thought she went to New York for college?* he wondered as a chill settled in his heart. If Bella was here, he can only imagine what kind of poisonous things she could have sprouted at Heather. He wished Heather called him... he wished he met her before he left.

"Bella came home for the short break..." mom answered.

"The one I didn't come for!" Nathan groaned.

"This was my fault! I promised Heather I'd come see her during that break and I didn't! Bella must have told her some nonsense! Heather almost died because of me!" he lamented.

"Nathan stop that! It's not your fault. We don't know for sure about what happened. There are rumours that her father left home too. So that might have had something to do with her decision. Don't jump into conclusions!" Himalie was firm with him.

"What? Why would he do that?"

"No one knows..." Mom sighed.

"That child deserved better than the treatment she got from them... even as a kid," Himalie seemed to know more.

"What do you mean, Himalie?"

"I don't know how much she's told you Nathan, but she

really had a sad childhood with her mother leaving, her father's neglect, a crazy uncle who almost..." Himalie stopped herself. "Anyway, that's all in the past. Good thing is now she has a new family," Himalie smiled.

Mom also smiled but she looked strangely at Nathan.

"New family?"

"She was adopted by someone when she was at the hospital... we got to see her once before she gained consciousness but when we went back, the hospital said she left with a new family."

"She's never spoken of any other family with me..." Nathan was suspicions.

"The people at the hospital said they were bound by the patient's wish for privacy and could not reveal any more information. All they said was she was adopted, and the new family took her home."

"WHERE?" Nathan suddenly understood why her mother looked strangely at him.

"We don't know. They won't tell us," Mom sighed.

"But MOM! How would I...? How can I...?" Nathan felt himself sink into his chair as the realization hit him.

He would never see Heather again!

It was close to two in the afternoon. There was a gentle breeze stirring up dead leaves on the sidewalk. It was hot and humid, yet Nathan felt none of that but rage as he waited outside Oceans International for Mikesh to come. He was the lion and Mikesh was the dirty little rat he was going to tear up. Nathan didn't know what exactly happened with Heather and Mikesh but he sensed it had something to do with her decision to jump off that bridge. He was going to find out exactly what Mikesh did... even if it meant...

Wait, there's Mikesh! his thoughts were interrupted as he noticed Mikesh's tall figure emerge into his view.

"Nathan!" Mikesh saw him before Nathan could get to him. His face paled and his body tensed. He looked afraid. *He should be,* Nathan thought as he slowly approached Mikesh. Nathan stopped when he stood facing Mikesh.

"What did you do?" he asked slowly, pausing in between each word, his tone making it clear that he did not have patience for nonsense.

"Dude... it wasn't my fault!" Mikesh looked nervous. He knew exactly what Nathan was asking him about.

"What.... did.... you do.... to Heather?"

"I was looking out for her! Honestly! I liked her! She's a good girl!"

"You? You were looking out for her? Is that what you were doing when you took these photos?" Nathan's eyes flashed with rage as he shoved his phone into Mikesh's face. Mikesh didn't need to see them to remember.

"Dude... we were just having fun! I didn't force her into anything. She came by herself. I swear!"

"SHE wouldn't have come if YOU didn't ask her to!" Nathan sneered.

"It took me a month to get her to come! She was so fixed on you!"

"What do you mean?"

"She thought you hated her and that's why you left without saying goodbye... at least that's what she was going on about when she was drunk."

"I hated her?"

"Something about hating her for liking you..."

"What? That's ridiculous... why would I?" Nathan was confused. He thought she was angry with him, thinking he led her on.

Mikesh chuckled. "I guess you actually cared for her."

Nathan's eyes narrowed. "She was my best friend!"

"I thought she was just your little project. You were just controlling her" Mikesh sneered.

Nathan glared, "I never tried to control her."

"You were just like my dad. He was a control freak, only caring about his image – never really about us. He always told us what to do... what not to do... just like you! Just like the way you did to us when you were a prefect and just like the way you did to Heather when you guys were apparently 'friends'. I hated you for that!"

"Heather always did what she wanted with me. I never controlled her," Nathan insisted; he finally understood why Mikesh always seemed to hate him.

"I just wanted Heather to be free. I wanted to give her a taste of freedom... to choose for herself what she wanted," Mikesh's expression changed. He looked at him pleadingly. He looked like he meant it and really wanted Nathan to believe him. Mikesh didn't seem to be lying.

"I believe you..." Nathan sighed, "but... I still don't understand what went wrong?"

"Bella..." Mikesh sighed, "I honestly didn't know how far she was going to take it when I agreed to help her."

Nathan's anger stirred up again.

"Help her with what?" he asked menacingly.

"It was all a plan you see…" Mikesh shuddered, "I can't believe I'm telling you all this."

Nathan's eyes narrowed.

Mikesh looked down, trying to avoid his gaze.

"Dude… I honestly didn't know she wanted to hurt Heather."

"Tell me what happened?" Nathan spoke through gritted teeth. He knew Bella had something to do with all this. His entire body felt cold as he waited to hear what horror Bella unleashed upon Heather while he was not there to protect her.

I failed her. Nathan couldn't resist the thought that crossed his mind.

Mikesh confessed everything to Nathan, "Bella got me to spill my drink on Heather to separate the two of you… she said she wanted to get revenge on you, Nathan, for rejecting her rudely… or something like that. She didn't say anything about wanting to hurt Heather – honestly!"

"So, you were 'Bella's' date that night?"

"Yeah… I was just glad to get a chance to have some fun with you guys one last time before you went off to college… while I'm still here…"

Nathan almost felt sorry for Mikesh.

"She said she had something to tell you without Heather knowing it, to get her revenge and that's why she wanted you alone. Sorry dude, you weren't my favourite person and taking revenge on you didn't sound too bad at that point."

Nathan rolled his eyes.

"Anyway, I saw Heather leaving and she didn't look okay, so I asked Bella why she looked upset."

"Since when did you care about Heather?" Nathan was truly

surprised that Mikesh showed concern for anyone other than himself.

Mikesh fidgeted a little, "She was kind dude. I spilled a drink on her pretty blue dress at the graduation dance! I've seen countless girls go crazy over spilt drinks on their outfits in house parties – this was *the* dance! I didn't think she'd be so kind to me... I really expected her to go berserk, slap me or insult me! I was shocked when she said 'it's okay... I can wash it up'!"

Nathan almost smiled at the memory. He was angry with Mikesh for trying to charm his way out, but *I guess I assumed wrong,* he thought. Out loud to Mikesh he said, "That's the kind of girl she is..."

"Exactly, dude... I've never met someone like her before. That's why I wanted to get to know her – which didn't work out because YOU pinned me to the wall." Mikesh's eyes flashed in anger.

"You spilled juice on her Mikesh... I was angry on her behalf. Anyway, when you talked to Bella at the dance, what did she say?"

"She told me Heather was upset because you were trying to get her to do something she didn't want to do."

"I never...!" Nathan started to protest but Mikesh cut in, "I know now that you care too much about her to try to force Heather into anything, but at that time I thought you were no different from my dad. So I assumed you were a jerk to try to force such a sweet girl to do things she didn't want to do... Then Bella said she had a plan to help Heather... to free her from your control – so I agreed to help her."

Nathan started to get a gist of Bella's plan.

Mikesh continued, "She told me to wait till you were gone off for college and try to get Heather to come for some parties and post photos of us doing things together on Facebook – without telling Heather. She told me to tag you in them and make you believe that Heather no longer wanted you around because she had me…"

Nathan grimaced as he remembered the photos, "Of course Heather wouldn't know or find out about any of this since she's not on Facebook".

"Exactly! I loved the plan because I wanted to get to know Heather and I got the chance to hurt you at the same time!" Mikesh sneered.

I don't think we'll get along after all, Nathan thought to himself.

"What I didn't know was that Bella wanted to use these photos to hurt Heather too. She told me you'd be too disgusted by Heather after seeing the photos because you're such a prig and leave Heather alone… giving her the freedom I wanted her to have…but I didn't think she'd actually tell that to Heather to hurt her. She went and told her that I posted those photos!" Mikesh clutched his head in dismay.

Understanding dawned on Nathan; "She told Heather that I must hate her after seeing the photos?"

"Yeah… worse actually. I told Heather the photos were just for me… so when Bella told her that I posted them on Facebook and tagged you, she made it sound like it was MY intention to hurt her… Heather was so upset. When she came to confront me, she was crying!" Mikesh's expression changed as if he was remembering something very unpleasant. "Bella told her that I never wanted to be friends with her in the first place, that I was just using her to get revenge on you and posted those photos on Facebook. She showed them to her as proof and of course Heather believed her."

"So, in the end, you got played too?" Nathan sneered.

"I guess..." Mikesh sighed. "This was around the time you were supposed to come home for break and Bella somehow found out that you wouldn't come."

Nathan's thoughts began to whirl, "Don't tell me?!"

"Yeah... Bella told Heather that the reason you didn't come back was because you hated her like her mom hated her, for what she had become... she had chosen to fall beneath your standards so you'd never want to see her again because she was no longer good enough to be your friend."

Nathan felt weak as he realized the extent of Bella's manipulation. Everything was planned out from the start and he conveniently fell into her trap! *She got* me *to feel guilty and made Heather feel like I hated her to drive a wedge between us at the dance. Then she used this photo ruse to make Heather feel like I condemned and hated her!* Knowing Heather's past, he could only imagine the pain she must have endured. "I never thought that way... when I saw the photos, I was just worried for her..." and then he grudgingly admitted, "and maybe a little jealous of you being so close to her."

"I dunno, dude, even I believed what Bella said – even though I hated her for making me a bad guy... you didn't say anything on Facebook – plus you actually didn't come home..."

"That's got nothing to do with this!" Nathan shouted – frustrated at how well Bella played her cards and tricked them all.

"Okay, chill dude!" Mikesh tried to calm him. "I guess when Heather's dad left it was all she could take..."

"Yeah... what was that about?"

"Well you know how Heather always got good grades yeah?"

"Of course, she studied hard because that's one thing her father was proud of her for... wait... did her grades drop?"

"Yeah... I guess she couldn't focus with all of this drama going on and her grades dropped. She failed English."

"English? But she's so good at it!"

"I dunno, dude. I wouldn't have cared. I tried to tell her when I found out that it's not a big deal, but she just looked at me with these hollow, accusing eyes and said, 'you don't understand' and left! That was the last I saw of her."

Nathan understood exactly what she felt. It is hard to accept failing a subject you're good at. "But what's this got to do with her dad leaving?"

"Well... it looked like her dad found out about the grade and got into a rage. The neighbours said they heard him shouting. He stormed out of the house with his luggage and Heather must have assumed he was leaving her for good."

"Was he?"

"Well... one of my pals Dasun... he's friends with Sheran... this guy who works with Heather's dad... after we heard about what happened at the bridge, I got him to find out what happened to Heather's dad."

Nathan found himself reluctantly admiring Mikesh's resourcefulness.

"Sheran told Dasun that Heather's dad got fired from the job and was planning to leave town to look for work somewhere else. He registered Heather to an orphanage because he couldn't take care of her anymore."

"But he didn't say any of that to Heather?"

"Exactly! He arranged for the orphanage to pick her up from home later on."

Nathan realized why Heather would have been pushed to take her own life. The weight of the actual and perceived rejection she must have felt would have been too heavy... definitely too heavy for her to bear alone.

"I wish I was here for her," Nathan muttered.

Mikesh looked away and for the first time, found himself agreeing with Nathan.

If Nathan was there, things definitely would have turned out differently.

Thunder rumbled in the distance. The windows were shut, and Bella watched the rain drops gently patter on to the glass, slowly making their way down, leaving behind a trail of tiny drops of water.

She loved thunderstorms as long as she was inside a warm, cosy house. She hated getting wet and especially, the cold.

Bet Heather felt cold and wet when she jumped.

She shivered as the thought crossed her mind.

Even though Bella was thousand miles away from home, living the life she always wanted through being an undergraduate, the horrid news reached her, carried on the wings of the Sri Lankan gossip network she couldn't avoid– also known as her illustrious elder sister. Bella thought it was a cruel joke and refused to take it seriously, until she read an extremely rude message Mikesh had sent, suggesting that SHE was the cause of Heather's unfortunate decision.

At first, Bella disagreed but as the days went by, guilt and shame kept knocking on the door to her heart. They were very uninvited guests.

I never expected her to get THAT hurt.... I just wanted Heather to learn a lesson... Heather and Nathan...

She felt an odd uncomfortable feeling. *I can never do anything right!*

Memories flooded her mind as she remembered her parents praising her elder sister for getting yet another prize for God knows what. Bella always felt like she was the second best at home. It was only at school that she felt seen, heard and accomplished. She was the queen at school, not her sister... not anyone else... until Heather came along.

First the auditions... then snatching Nathan from right under her nose! Was it that wrong of her to try and teach Heather a lesson? She couldn't do anything to her 'precious' elder sister without getting a thorough yelling from her parents... but when it came to Heather and Nathan, who was there to stop her? At least she could do something about them! She found an outlet to release her bottled up anger when she planned her revenge on Heather and felt free for the first time when she carried it out. Sadly, the freedom and relief were short lived. Ever since she heard the news from her sister, Bella lived in constant fear that she would be accused of murder if Heather died. Her guilt tore at her with claws that cut deep. She never knew that regret and guilt could be this painful.

For the millionth time Bella wondered if she could have done things differently?

As always, the universe responded with a deafening silence.

CHAPTER EIGHT

The water was still and clear. Heather could see her reflection perfectly even from high up on the rickety metal bridge. It was a few hours after school ended so the cement path lined with trees was isolated. Not many took this route.

Heather felt dead inside. She lost all hope when Nathan left without saying goodbye. She was sure it was because he hated her for liking him. She clung on to the small ember of hope, that when he came back home for break, she could apologize for her feelings and tell him that she wouldn't let it be a burden to him, but then Mikesh... she felt the pain in her heart that had become her constant companion these days intensify. She couldn't believe how Mikesh could betray her like that! He was kind and good to her, so much so that it almost took away the sting of Nathan's hatred towards her... but to find out it was all to get revenge on Nathan? She was used to hurt Nathan and she didn't even know! She was so stupid! So what else was new? No wonder her parents left her... they couldn't bear to face the fact that they gave birth to such a stupid, ugly, useless child like her. Nathan was the only one who truly saw value in her and now she'd gone and ruined things with him too. He was never going to like her or want to be friends with her now. Heather clutched her head remembering Nathan pinning Mikesh on the wall. She KNEW Nathan didn't like Mikesh – why was she so STUPID enough to go to parties with him? How could she be so stupid to think he'd take those photos and not post them anywhere? Heather hated herself. She was truly worthless. She couldn't do anything right. She failed English! That was her easiest subject! Nothing she did ever turned out right. No one she loved ever loved her back. She was useless. A waste of space. Why was she even living? What was the point of living if nothing changed? All her life, things had just gone from bad to worse. She had nothing to look forward to. She had no family, how was she going to survive? On charity? But who would care for her? Who'd bother to give her any money to live on?

Looking at her red eyes and blotched face staring back at her from the water, Heather despised herself. She didn't want to live. She didn't want to keep enduring the pain she suffered for so long. Nathan was her only joy and she ruined things with him too. She seemed to have a knack for ruining things. There was nothing good about her. She was just a glitch in the system, a dot in history; insignificant. No one would even care or even notice whether she was there or not. So what was the point of living? Why bother enduring this pain?

Suddenly, Heather became aware that she was balancing herself at the edge of the railing. She somehow managed to climb over it. There was nothing between her and the water. She couldn't swim. If she fell... she'd be dead within minutes.

All your pain and suffering will end in minutes if you just jump... you won't ever have to endure pain again... ever, she heard a voice whisper within her. She felt a sob rise within her as she thought of the truth of those words. She slowly leaned forward... until she was no longer on the bridge.

She was falling!

As the water loomed closer and seemed to rise to meet her and embrace her, fear gripped her heart. *I can't swim! Oh God! I can't swim! I'll die!*

As she plunged into the cold lake, she struggled to keep her head above water, but she kept sinking. Water kept filling up her nose, mouth, everywhere! She was cold, and the deathly currents of water seem to enfold her. She couldn't breathe! The light around her began to fade and she felt the water engulf her completely. She was sinking. She was going to die. *Just let go. You don't have to fight. It'll be all over soon.* she heard a voice whisper in her mind. Heather felt weak. She gave in. She stopped struggling yet just before everything faded to black, she saw a bearded man looking down at her through the water.

His face was the kindest, most beautiful face she had ever seen and there was a glow about him – a bright glow that outshone her darkness. "Do you want to live?" He asked. Heather somehow heard his voice within her. She wasn't sure how he did that. His voice was gentle and soft – filled with warmth, love and compassion. "If I give you another chance my dear...a chance to be with me... would you like to live?" Gazing at the eyes of this stranger, Heather realized she did want to live... if it meant she could be with him. For some reason she felt he would keep her safe. She tried to say "yes" but she couldn't form the words. She couldn't feel her lips. They were not moving even though she wanted them to. He started reaching for her. She tried to reach out to him with any remaining strength she had but her arms were limp. They were not responding. Before she could reach him, everything went black.

Beep. Beep. Beep. The sound was annoying. Was that the alarm clock?

Heather groggily tried to reach for the offending noise – to switch it off but she couldn't move well. She felt very weak and her hands felt odd, like something was attached to it.

"Doctor! I think she's awake!" a female voice spoke near her.

"Doctor? Was she in a hospital?" Heather wondered as she slowly opened her eyes. The brightness of white fluorescent light almost blinded her as her eyes took time to adjust. She looked around and took in her surroundings. There were several beds lined up near her. There were green curtains around each bed, some far from her were drawn close to give its occupants some privacy while others were open. The floor was tiled in white and the walls were painted white near the ceiling and green closer to the tiles. Most of the beds near her were empty, but few further away had people lying down or sleeping with IV drips attached to their hands. She was in a hospital ward, Heather realized. Her hand felt odd because it was attached to an IV drip too. There was a nurse beside her bed and as Heather tried to straighten up, a man with a stethoscope appeared. "So that's the doctor!" Heather thought sleepily.

"Hi, Heather, how do you feel?"

"Um... Okay" Heather croaked. Her throat was dry.

"Give her some water," the doctor instructed the nurse.

"Do you remember anything that happened?" the doctor asked her gently as he slowly did some physical checks.

Heather was a little confused. Why was she in the hospital? Last thing she remembered was... and then, like a rush, her memories flooded in.

"Oh..."

"What happened?" the doctor continued to talk to her gently.

"I... I jumped!" Heather muttered, with her eyes cast down.

"Do you remember anything else that happened after you jumped?"

She did.

"I saw someone. A man with a beard. He looked very kind and I just felt so much love from him."

"Okay... where did you see him?"

"I was drowning... I was under water. He was on the water's surface, looking down at me and then he stretched his hand towards me and I tried to grab it... that's all I remember".

"Heather, you must have been hallucinating because that's impossible. You were in the middle of the lake. How can a man be on the water? Unless he was in a boat?"

"I didn't see a boat," she mumbled.

"Doctor, there was no boat in the footage," the nurse whispered.

"But that's impossible!" The doctor sounded exasperated.

"Sounds like a miracle to me!" one of the patients in the bed next to her responded.

The nurse nodded in agreement.

"There's no such things as miracles!" the doctor insisted. "There's got to be a scientific way to explain this."

"Well, with all respect sir, just because you don't want to believe in miracles doesn't mean they don't happen," the patient gently replied.

"Doctor, how do you explain how she was saved in the first place if it wasn't for a miracle? You saw the CCTV footage from the bridge!" the nurse seemed to agree with the patient.

"Excuse me? Can someone tell me if you know who that

bearded man is? I'd like to talk to him. He saved my life, didn't he?"

The nurse exchanged a glance with the doctor.

"Hun, there was no one."

"What? What do you mean? Then how did I...?"

"The footage shows you jumping from the bridge and sinking. Then it was like the water in the lake started forming waves, just like in the sea and those waves brought you ashore".

"But... it was still! The lake! There wasn't even a ripple! I could see my reflection perfectly before I... before I did it!" Heather insisted.

"I'm just telling you what the CCTV footage shows."

"Then who was the bearded man?" Heather wondered out loud.

"I think you had an encounter with Jesus," the patient chimed in.

The doctor rolled his eyes, but the nurse seemed to agree. "That would actually make sense... He probably got the waves to save you!"

"Jesus?" Heather wondered out loud. Nathan's family prayed to Jesus. Jackson and Himalie would sometimes talk about him, but who was this Jesus? Was he a 'god' to get waves to form on water to save her? Was he so powerful that he could walk on water and be invisible from CCTV cameras?

"We live in the 21ˢᵗ century! Jesus is dead. He's not going around rescuing people," the doctor interrupted.

"He died, and He rose again! He's still living," the patient answered.

"Doctor, how else do you explain the phone call?"

"What phone call?" Heather was clueless.

"Someone called the emergency number for the ambulance several minutes before you jumped, according to the camera recording, so our team actually got to you just seconds after you came ashore. None of the emergency team members saw anyone around! It was perfect timing! If they called the hospital after you jumped, even if we left immediately, by the time we got there, you'd be dead on the shore!"

That's crazy! How did anyone know I was going to jump? Heather wondered.

"Are you sure you didn't tell anyone?" the doctor looked at her suspiciously.

"No! I swear! I wasn't planning on doing it... it's just there were some stuff and I was just overwhelmed, and it just happened..."

"You couldn't take it anymore?" the nurse interrupted.

Heather nodded as tears welled up in her eyes.

"There you see, Doctor? You must admit it. It was a miracle! Did you know that the police tried to trace the phone call but had no luck?"

"Yeah... they said it was untraceable right?"

"Exactly! You got to admit it, Doctor, God might actually be real!"

"Might!" the doctor sighed and refused to give in. "Heather, I'll be back to check on you. You're a very lucky girl to have a second chance to live like this. Please don't ever try to take your life again, okay?" he gently chided her, as he got ready to leave.

Tears streamed down Heather's face. The nurse handed her a tissue, held her hand in a warm grip and smiled. "Praise God you're alive! Nothing is worth taking your life. I'm sure there's so much you can do in this world. You need to find the will to live, okay?"

"Nurse!" the doctor called for her from the door.

"Coming!" she hurried off with a final smile and a wave to her.

Heather sniffled into her tissue.

She couldn't believe what she just heard. It sounded so surreal. She tried to process and make sense of it.

The patient on the next bed suddenly sat up straight on his bed. Heather turned to look at him, nose red and eyes swollen with tears. She must look like a clown she thought as she observed her only neighbour for the time she'll be spending here. The other patients were too far in the ward for her to communicate.

He was older than her with streaks of white hair shining on his well-combed head. He wore black and gold rimmed glasses that couldn't hide the sharpness of his keen and intelligent eyes that gave his face a very professional look. Even though he was smiling kindly to her right now, he had the aura of a powerful man (even while on a sick bed) who you just don't mess with. His beard was neatly trimmed, and he looked like the epitome of a healthy person. *I wonder why he's in the hospital when he looks so well?* Heather wondered to herself.

"So... you're Heather? Is that right?" the patient asked her with barely contained excitement.

"Yeah... I'm sorry, I didn't catch your name."

"I'm David Harold Rodrigo. I go by Harold," he smiled.

"I had a teacher called David once! He was one of my favourites!" Heather eased. Harold seems familiar. Almost like she's seen him before.

"Really? Well I hope we get along since you'll be stuck with me until one of us gets to go!" he grinned.

Despite her usual reservation with strangers, Heather found herself liking Harold. It was the same warm feeling she had with Nathan – not the attraction, but just a sense of safety and trust.

"So, how was it like? Meeting Jesus?" Harold asked and now she could see what Harold was excited about.

"I dunno. I honestly don't know anything about Him. Maybe I was just hallucinating."

"You were not! Your rescue story sounded like the kind of thing Jesus would do. I'm pretty sure you encountered Him!" Harold sounded confident.

"Okay... well... He was beautiful. I actually can't remember His features, but I just got this sense that He was beautiful and kind. He was glowing! There was this light about him that was so bright! Everything was going dark around me, but His light was so bright, I just felt warm even when the water was so cold… and love... I felt so much love..." Tears sprung up in her eyes again as she remembered that moment when for the first time in her life, she felt overwhelmingly loved. She has never experienced that kind of love from anyone. Not even Nathan.

Harold smiled, waiting for her to continue.

"It made me want to be with Him. It made me wanted to try and reach Him, so I could be with Him, loved by Him... but I couldn't reach Him. His hand was outstretched to me, but I guess I didn't have enough strength to reach Him," Heather sighed. "He gave me a choice... He asked if I would want to live again if He gave me a second chance... to live with Him..."

"You know, I think Jesus gave you the chance to choose Him. When you tried to reach Him – even though you failed, I think He saw your heart that wanted to come to Him. So even when you passed out of consciousness, Jesus probably grabbed hold of you and did that miracle to save your life! I think He left enough signs to show you that it was Him, so you won't doubt it!" Harold spoke with conviction.

"Who is Jesus?" Heather asked Harold who seem to know a lot about Him.

"You haven't heard of Him?" Harold looked amazed as Heather shook her head.

"I've only heard bits and pieces. Never enough to actually 'know' who He is..."

"Well I don't think anyone actually 'knows' Jesus fully – He is God you know... No man can fully comprehend God – there is so much mystery to Him. But if I was to simply describe Jesus to you, He's the Son of God who died to save mankind from sin, curses and death. Then He came back to life and now lives forever!"

"So, is He a God or *like* a God?"

"He *is* God! The only God there is in this universe!"

"But you just said He is the Son of God?" Heather was confused.

"Ah... this gets some people confused. Okay, see, God exists in three forms: Father, Son and the Holy Spirit, but He is only one God!"

Heather was still confused, "How can He be one if He is three? That makes no sense."

Harold thought a little and then seemed to get an idea.

"Have you studied chemistry at school?"

"Yeah..."

"Okay, water... what is it made out of?"

"Hydrogen and oxygen" Heather replied automatically.

"Do you know the chemical formula for it?"

"H_2O, right?" Heather replied confused where Harold was

taking this. "What's that got to do with God?"

"Well... beside the fact that sometimes we describe God as the living water, I just wanted to help you understand how God exists in three forms but is One God using water as an example."

"Okay.... so, water is H2O but that doesn't explain anything."

"Right let me get to it. Heather, tell me, when you drink water what kind of substance is it? What's its state?"

"Liquid?" Heather replied raising an eyebrow. She really didn't see where Harold was taking this.

"Okay... but when you put it in the freezer what happens to this liquid water?"

"It freezes!"

"Yeah, so will it remain in the liquid state then?"

"Of course not! It's ice – so it is a solid!"

"Exactly! Okay, now think Heather, if you heat water past the boiling point, what happens?"

"It becomes vapor!" Heather was starting to get frustrated, "Seriously Harold, are you making fun of me? I know my chemistry! What I don't know is where you're going with this!"

Harold chuckled.

"Right, so now you said water exists as liquid, solid and vapor or gas – yeah?"

Resigning, Heather nodded in agreement.

"So, in all three instances was it still H2O or did it change and become something else?"

"Of course not! Water is H2O! That doesn't change whether its ice, liquid water or water vapour!" even as she said those words, understanding dawned on Heather.

"God is the same!" Harold smiled, knowing he finally got

through to Heather. "He is one God even though He exists in three forms, just like water only has that one chemical formula – H2O, whether it exists as solid, liquid or gas"

"Wow! That's deep!" Heather was amazed at the analogy.

"That's the God we believe in! He created everything. He's so good and He's so full of love – like you already experienced."

Heather let that sink in but a thought that unsettled her crept in and she blurted it out. "If God is so good and if He's so full of love, why did He let me suffer so much? I never did anything to deserve it!" Heather felt anger suddenly rise inside of her.

"I could try to give a very general answer for you, but I might be able to give a better answer if you don't mind sharing your story with me," Harold gently asked her.

Heather looked at this kind man who genuinely seemed to care and seemed to have answers for her questions. Maybe he could help her understand 'why' and give her a reason for her struggles. Heather shared her story with him, from the very beginning. She told him about her mom leaving, being neglected by her father, uncle Charith, the bullying at school, Bella, Nathan, Mikesh... she told him everything and Harold patiently listened only interrupting her if he needed to clarify something.

"So now, tell me... If God is so good, why did he let me suffer so much? I didn't do anything wrong. Okay, maybe when Nathan and Dad left me, that was my fault, but Mom? Uncle Charith? The bullying?"

Harold sighed.

"I'm so sorry for the painful childhood you've had to endure Heather. I could understand how this pain was too overwhelming for you to handle alone, but... even in the middle of the terrible way your family treated you and even the bullying, I can see

God's goodness and love for you!"

"What? How?" Heather was truly confused. Was he mad? Where is there any goodness or love of God for her in all that she endured?

"Well... even though your mom hated you, treated you bad and left you in such a horrible way, she still gave birth to you. She didn't abort you. God's goodness and love for you is there as he protected your life. Then until very recently, your father – even though he wasn't perfect in caring for you, still provided for you. You had a house to live in, food to eat, clothes to wear. You had the chance to go to school. These are things that some children don't have."

There was truth in his words. Heather just never looked at it that way.

Harold continued, "Even when your uncle was going to take advantage of you, God protected you by getting the police to rescue you right on time! When you didn't go to school, He got your neighbours to tutor you and even when your classmates bullied you, God showed you His love through teachers who helped you and later through your friend, Nathan! Then finally, when your choices almost led to your death at that lake, God's goodness and love for you was so great – He actually showed Himself to you and rescued you!"

It took Heather a few minutes to take it all in. She never looked at things this way. Harold truly saw everything differently. He gave her a fresh perspective and made her feel less like a victim of her circumstances.

"I get what you're saying," Heather finally replied. "There's still something I don't understand. Why didn't God stop them in the first place? Why was Mom so mean? Why was uncle Charith like that? Then the kids at school... how could He let them be so cruel if He is so good?"

"I won't claim to have all the answers Heather but from my understanding, there's something you need to know about the nature of evil in this world to get an answer to those questions. That would take us back to the story of creation."

"Story of creation? What's that?"

"You've never read a Bible, have you?"

Heather shook her head.

"Well, the first chapter in the Bible is the story of creation. It talks about how God created the universe, all creatures, trees and us humans. Then He looked at what He created and said, 'it was good.'"

"So, you're trying to say that everything – including all humans are good?" Heather scoffed.

"In the very beginning yes, it was ALL good but that's when problems started. Things changed."

"Okay... what happened?"

"Well some other chapters in the Bible talks about an enemy – Lucifer was an angel who was too proud. His heart became evil. Him and his angels – we call them demons now – they went against God. They hated God and everything God created. They wanted to destroy it all! They especially hated humans because God created us in His image. When they see us, they see the God they hate, in us."

"This sounds like a fairy tale," Heather laughed, even as she felt goosebumps.

"Maybe... but you'll see how it all makes sense"

"You really believe all this stuff? Angels? Demons? God?"

"With all my heart!"

"But you can't see them! How do you know they're real?"

"What are you breathing right now?"

"Air"

"Okay, what's in the air that all living creatures need to live?"

"Oxygen?"

"Okay, so do you think there's oxygen here right now in the air?"

"Of course!" Heather laughed

"How do you know? You can't see it!"

"But I'm alive because I'm breathing it. So I know it's there!"

"Exactly!"

That's when understanding dawned on Heather again.

"Just because I don't see them doesn't mean they're not real, we can know they're real by external circumstances, conditions or things that happen due to their existence! Interesting! I never thought of things this way!" Heather learned so much from Harold just by talking with him for a few minutes.

Harold chucked at Heather's excitement. "I'm glad you're opening your eyes! So... where was I?"

"Lucifer... the demons..."

"Ah, Yes! We also call Lucifer Satan, by the way. Anyway, the first two humans on earth, Adam and Eve, they had everything they ever needed to survive. God walked with them, talked with them, they were able to see God too! God gave man a gift of free will – because he didn't want us to be robots doing everything he says out of obligation – because we 'have to'. He wanted us to choose to obey because we loved Him. God wanted us to have a relationship with Him as sons and daughters. That's why like I said before; He created us like Himself, in His image. So, He told Adam and Eve to enjoy life in the garden where they were – eat anything except fruit from this one tree."

"Don't tell me, they ate from that tree?"

"Yes! Satan tricked them – well the Bible actually says a snake tricked them – but usually we believe that this is a metaphor for Satan though some say Satan influenced the snake, but that's not what's important… what's important is Adam and Eve were tricked into believing that they were not like God."

"Even though you said they were created in God's image and were already like God?"

"Yes, exactly! They were tricked into thinking that they had to eat from the forbidden tree to be like God. So, they disobeyed God, eating the forbidden fruit and sin entered the world," Harold sighed.

"Sin?"

"That's when you do something God says not to do. Missing the mark or not meeting God's requirements… Sin is not good. It destroys what is good, which is what happened. When sin entered the world, God's creation, which was good and in perfect harmony, was destroyed. Many people point this out to be the root cause of some of the chaos in this world – even natural disasters. Sin also corrupts man when it grows in a man's heart. Generations after Adam and Eve, people became increasingly sinful and evil as the first sin of Adam and Eve passed down to all mankind and so – people were separated from God because of their sin and the free will they had to choose sin over choosing God. So that's why those people were cruel to you. They had sin in their hearts and they were using the God given gift of free will to make bad choices to hurt you and follow their evil plans, but God was so good to protect you from them."

"So, are you saying God will never stop people from doing wrong things because of this gift of free will?"

"Heather, you need to understand this first. God is not the one to cause evil – that's usually Satan or it happens as a result of the broken, sinful nature of our world now. So, you can't blame God for evil. He allows certain things however, because He sees the future. Sometimes some of the cruel, painful things we endure makes us stronger and helps us in our future. Many times, there is a purpose behind our pain, at the very least you will meet someone someday that you can help because of the painful experiences you've had. There's a story in the Bible of a man called Joseph. Joseph was his father's favourite, he did no wrong, but his jealous brothers sold him off to slavery. He was taken to Egypt, where he was accused wrongly and put in prison. However, in the end, from prison, he was raised up to a place of authority in Egypt where ultimately he was able to help many people during a time of famine – even the brothers who wronged him."

"Wow... that's so encouraging! I didn't think that any of the things I suffered through might help someone someday."

"It's a difficult idea for people to understand or accept. No one likes to go through painful things – even if it is for the good of others. That's why God interferes and puts a stop to certain wrong things even when you chose it, but if something bad does happen, we can always trust God to use it all for good in the end. He always gives us the strength and support we need to endure any difficult experience we face."

"Just like He gave me Himalie and Jackson, my teachers at school... and Nathan..."

"Exactly! Do you understand now, why you can't blame God for people's cruelty and evil?"

"I guess... it's a lot to take in though."

"Your head must be about to burst."

"A little... I guess...." Heather smiled. "Well, I'm glad if what I went through might help someone else someday," but there was another question that nagged her.

"Hey, Harold... you said we're separated from God because of sin yeah?"

"Yeah..."

"But you said God created us to be in relationship with him. So, how's that working out for God then?"

"Very sharp!" Harold smiled. "You asked a very good question. That's why God sent Jesus to die for us. Every single human after Adam and Eve was born as sinners into this world and are by default separated from God because of their sinful nature. There's no amount of good works that you do, that makes you good enough for God. His standards are so high, humanly it is impossible to live a sin free life by our strength alone. So, God came to earth as Jesus, lived a life without any sin and died on the cross for every single human's sins – past, present and future!"

"Why did he have to die?"

"The punishment for sin is death! Ah! I forgot to tell you that. Adam and Eve would have lived forever if they didn't sin. Humanity started dying only because of sin."

"So, Jesus took the punishment for all of our sins when he died on the cross?"

"Exactly! He went through excruciating pain, suffering and death (when he did no wrong to deserve any of it) and then three days later he conquered death and came to life again, restoring us to God and giving hope to all humanity."

"Hope of eternal life after death? Wow!"

"Yeah! That's why I love Jesus so much! You were blessed to

get a chance to see Him!"

Heather realized then that Harold was right. She was blessed. That was the first time she ever thought she was. All what Harold said made sense and she had encountered this Jesus at the brink of death – which proved that He was real!

"So how do you have a relationship with God?"

Harold looked excited. "Very simple. You must first confess your sins to God – that means you tell God about all the wrongs you've done as you remember them and ask Him to forgive you, choosing not to do those wrongs things again. You must believe that Jesus died to forgive those sins and rose three days later to give you eternal life and then you choose to invite Him in to your heart and make Him Lord God over your life. When you do this, you're choosing to follow Him from that point on."

"I just have to believe in Jesus?"

"That definitely is the most important part... confess your sins, ask for forgiveness, repent, believe Jesus and invite Jesus to be Lord of your life."

Heather felt an excitement come over her.

"Do I have to go somewhere special to do it? Like a church?"

"Not at all! You can just pray and invite Jesus to your life anywhere you are."

"How do you pray?"

Harold chuckled. "Praying, from what I believe, is simply talking to God. So, you just talk to God like you're talking to me and then usually at the end we say 'in Jesus's name, Amen' – because it was Jesus's sacrifice that connects us to God."

"Okay..." Heather was excited but confused. She wanted to pray and invite this Jesus into her life but didn't know how to start. Harold seem to sense her confusion.

"Would you like to pray?" Harold looked at her questioningly.

"Yes! I want to know Jesus more!" Heather giggled. "I want to invite Him into my life! I want to follow Him as my Lord and saviour because He did actually rescue me from dying in that lake!"

All the worries, all her pain, all the memories she had suddenly felt far away – like it was from another place and time – like it happened to someone else. She just felt like a big door was going to open before her and she just needed to walk through it.

Harold looked just as excited as she was. His eyes shone with kindness towards her.

"Okay... to start off, why don't you confess your sins to God, ask Him to forgive you and choose not to do them again – in your heart"

"Do I have to say it out loud?" Heather suddenly felt nervous.

"No... That's up to you. You can say it in your heart if you want to."

"Okay..." Heather closed her eyes and shut out all distractions. For a moment there was nothing but silence, then words began to form in her mind.

"God... if you can hear me, I just wanted to say sorry for all of my sins. God you are the one in control of everything. I've undermined your authority when I decided to take my own life. It's not up to me to decide when my life should end, I'm sorry God. I hurt Nathan, I behaved badly with Mikesh and did things I shouldn't have done... I've lied about homework sometimes to Jackson and Himalie, I've been angry and offended people... God, I'm so sorry for my sins. I won't do them again. Please help me not to do them again. Please forgive me."

Heather opened her eyes, feeling a little foolish, yet at the same time felt like a huge weight was off of her back.

"Done?" Harold asked patiently.

"Yeah! Now what?"

"Just repeat after me…" Harold closed his eyes and slowly started a prayer. Heather closed her eyes and repeated the prayer when Harold stopped after each sentence.

They prayed like this:

"Dear heavenly Father, thank you for forgiving me of all of my sins – past, present and future. Jesus, I believe you died on a cross to set me free from my sins and you rose again in three days to give me eternal life. I turn my back on my sins and choose to live a new life surrendered to you. Please come into my life, be my Lord and saviour. Take complete control. I will follow you from now on. In Jesus's name I pray, Amen."

As she was praying, Heather felt warmth, as if a gentle warm breeze enveloped her. As soon as it came, it was gone but it felt like it took away any remaining weight she had in her life. For the first time in her life she truly felt light and free.

Harold continued to observe Heather. She was truly a smart, talented child with a lot of potential, very quick to learn. Even after accepting Jesus, she had so many questions and Harold took great care to answer each of them. She reminded him of his younger self. It would be a waste to let her go back to a surrounding that would only crush and diminish her. He decided to give her an opportunity to change her life just like his mentor in university gave him that opportunity. As a plan began to hatch in his mind, he chuckled at the reaction he would get, not only from the media – who always had something to say about everything whether it was true or not (just to get higher ratings), but also from Heather. She didn't know just how good God was to her by placing her in the same ward, right next to the one man with enough resources to change her life, overnight.

It was two days since Harold left and Heather was bored without his companionship. Despite their age difference, they got along well. She learned so much from him and he left her a Bible to read before he was discharged. Heather was killing time reading the Bible, thinking about God, life and what her future was going to be like. That was another reason why she missed Harold. She didn't have the chance to worry about her future when he was there. They'd be so busy talking.

Now that he was gone, and she didn't know whether she'd ever meet him again. (He said they would, but she assumed it was just him being kind). She kept wondering what would happen to her once she gets discharged.

Her recovery seemed satisfactory to the doctors, so she knew she would be discharged soon. What next? Where am I going to go? How will I survive? Dad's not home... what will I do? How can I pay the hospital bills?

Strangely, every time these worries came, she heard a whisper in her mind telling her not to worry... that things will work out because now God's in control of her life. It would bring her some peace and reassurance for a while but eventually she'd return to her worrying until at last, exhausted from her worrying, she'll just whisper to God, or pray as Harold called it, "Please... Please help me... I don't know how, but somehow, take care of me Jesus!"

"WHAT? You're adopting me?" Heather was shocked when Harold came to meet her, dressed in a neatly pressed black pin striped business suit. She felt a sense of authority and strength from Harold when he was with her as a patient in the hospital but, dressed in a business suit – Harold seemed to radiate power. The shock of Harold's new appearance and aura was nothing compared to the shock she felt when he announced his intention to adopt her.

"I wanted to contact your father about this, but I actually found out that he registered you to an orphanage before he left you... leaving all rights regarding you in the hands of the custodians... did you know that?"

Heather's eyes filled up with tears. "No," she whispered. So, dad did care enough to at least make sure she wouldn't be destitute.

"You have a choice before you Heather – go to the orphanage or come with me and be my daughter," Harold spoke to her gently.

"But why would you...? I'd be such a burden to you! You'll have to support me... pay for college..."

Harold coughed and interrupted her with twinkling eyes.

"You clearly don't know who I am, do you Heather?"

"You're David Harold Rodrigo... right?"

"Yes... and that doesn't ring any bells to you?"

She remembered thinking he looked familiar, but she couldn't quite figure out how.

"My public relations team won't be happy to hear this," Harold sighed.

"Are you someone I should know of?" Heather asked timidly, suddenly aware that she really didn't know much about Harold even though she pretty much told him her entire life story.

Harold chuckled.

"Its fine Heather. All you need to know is, if you choose to be my daughter and let me adopt you, I will take very good care of you. You will lack nothing but will have only the best of everything that I can give you." His kind eyes did not lie. He meant every word.

"I... I'd love to... you're an answered prayer! I guess God really does care for me!"

"Of course He does! Silly child!" Harold leaned forward and ruffled her hair and then straightening up, he said "I just have one condition though..."

"What is it?"

"I'm giving you an opportunity to start a new life, I'm giving you a new identity, so I need you to leave behind your old one. You have to let go of your past."

"Yeah... Sure! I'd be happy to!" Heather smiled.

"You'll have to change your name. Is that fine?" Harold spoke with concern.

"My name? You mean my last name, right?"

"No... your entire name"

"You're going to give me a new name?"

"Yup!" Harold's eyes twinkled with excitement.

"What will it be?"

"Your new name will be Arielle Davidson Rodrigo!"

"Davidson?"

"Yeah... like David's child... you know... thought that'll be cool to help you remember you're my daughter," Harold looked at her expectantly. "What do you think?"

"I like it!" Heather smiled.

"Arielle means lioness of Judah... I wanted your name to remind you that you are powerful now... you are not Heather, who was trodden down by others. I wanted your name to remind you that you're not only my daughter but that you are God's daughter too!" Harold explained.

He had clearly thought a lot about it.

Her real father hardly gave much thought to her... things were really going to change for her.

"Thank you, Harold, or should I call you dad now?" Heather teased.

Harold thought for a moment and smiled. "Whatever you're comfortable with."

Heather looked at Harold and realized she'd be honoured to have a father like him.

'Thanks... Dad..." she smiled.

Harold's eyes seemed to shine with love for her.

"You're welcome... Arielle."

CHAPTER NINE

Aᴿɪᴇʟʟᴇ ʟᴏᴏᴋᴇᴅ ᴀᴛ ʜᴇʀ ᴄʟᴏᴛʜᴇs and hesitated. The array of choices before her in the walk-in closet she now owned, overwhelmed her – not for the first time. She owned clothes that at one point she would have only dreamt of. They were all custom made to fit her perfectly by well-known designers. She remembered vaguely the time she had to dig into her mother's clothe pile to find a dress for the graduation dance. That seemed a million years ago... the life of someone else. Arielle firmly pushed back the memory. She had learned to do that since she came to live with Harold. She was no longer Heather from the past. She fully embraced her new identity – Arielle.

Refocusing on the issue at hand, Arielle wondered if she should go with the long red dress that would make her look elegantly mature or the shorter green dress that would highlight her youth?

Harold has invited a few guests over for a small Christmas dinner. She was required to be there to entertain the guests with her music and singing – a talent Harold immediately recognized within the first month of their relationship as father and daughter. He wasted no time in getting her a music instructor to teach her how to play the piano and guitar, as well as an instructor to give her voice training.

Four years ago, when Harold made the offer to adopt Arielle, she had no idea that she was going to become the daughter and inheritor of the third wealthiest man in the country. When she entered her new home, she was overwhelmed by the size of the mansion and the extent to which God had blessed her with this new identity.

There were many things to get used to. Her room was the size of her old living room and kitchen combined. It was huge. The indoors were tiled in marble and there were lush carpets that soothed her feet. She had a mini chandelier in her room in addition to the chandeliers that towered over other rooms in the mansion like the dining hall or near the main stairway at the entrance. The mansion was built in the manner of an old Victorian English house with modern necessities. She couldn't believe such a place existed in Colombo!

She was required to travel by their private vehicle for security purposes and there were many new etiquettes, manners and vocabulary for her to learn as she was representing Harold and his business conglomerate wherever she went. She was home-schooled for the remainder of her high school years by the best tutors Harold could find.

Harold took her with him for many company visits, explaining the various industries, their function, future plans and Arielle loved it. She felt like she has always been his daughter. True to his words he never let Arielle feel any lack.

At first, it was difficult for Arielle to believe that she could be the daughter of such an amazing powerful man, but Harold's constant encouragement, love and presence in her life eventually made the transition easier. Slowly Arielle transformed. Her former fears, insecurities and feelings of shame and unworthiness was erased by Harold's constant love and care but more importantly by his constant reminder to her about her identity in God.

Harold never missed church on Sunday. No matter how busy his schedule was, he always made time for Sunday church and to pray with her before bedtime. He answered any questions she had about God during that time and always reminded her that she was the lioness of God.

Slowly, she became less timid and grew bolder. Harold started giving her small responsibilities in the running of the household as he saw her confidence grow.

One of Arielle's favourite things to do together with Harold was their visits to charity organizations. Arielle loved how Harold didn't collect his wealth only for himself, but consciously distributed it to help those in need. He took the ability to help society through his influence and wealth, seriously. His motive behind it was not to improve his image with the public – which usually was the motive of many popular, wealthy people when they contribute to charity. He would always say that, "It's my duty to society, Arielle... God blesses us to be a blessing to others. Not to selfishly keep everything to ourselves. Always remember that."

During the first year of her adoption, Harold initiated a campaign to raise funds to improve public health institutions. He used his personal experiences at public and private hospitals in the country as an example and educated officials about the way people are treated differently in each. He emphasized that everyone deserved proper medical care and attention regardless of whether they have the money to go to a private hospital or they depend on the government for health care through public hospitals.

Watching Harold inspired Arielle. The way he used every resource to prudently improve his business as well as to help those in need, influenced Arielle greatly. She decided to be more like Harold and use whatever God gave her to help others.

After visiting the orphanage, she was going to live in if Harold didn't adopt her, Arielle's heart was burdened. These facilities needed more funds for upkeep and to take better care of the children.

So, Arielle wanted to use her musical ability to encourage people and use whatever she earned to support these children's homes and single parents who needed financial assistance because she remembered the struggle she faced while growing up with only her father.

Harold loved the idea and agreed to give her his fullest support. In fact, since then, he deliberately got her to entertain his important guests with influence, using her musical talents, giving her the exposure she needed, as well as the opportunity to practice singing in front of an audience.

"There will be a music producer at tonight's dinner party," Harold gave her a heads-up. "Who knows, if you blow his mind off with your talent, you might instantly get a contract," Harold teased her playfully.

"Dad! You're making me nervous!"

"Nervous? My little lioness?" Harold laughed, "I don't believe it! You're bold! You can do this!"

"Sometimes I wish I had your confidence in me, Dad." Arielle grinned.

"Just know who you are. You are God's princess and you are my daughter. You're set up to win! There's no way you will fail at anything!" Harold insisted.

"Thanks, Dad," Arielle replied as she soaked in the warmth

of those words. She decided to do her best and leave the rest in God's hands.

CHAPTER TEN

"**D**AD! I GOT IT!" ARIELLE exclaimed as she jumped up from the breakfast table with excitement.

Harold insisted on a specific breakfast routine. He believed that the start of the day determines how the rest of the day spans out. So, his routine was to wake up and spend time reading the Bible. Then, he would meet her at exactly half past seven in the morning at the base of the staircase downstairs. Arielle would give Harold a hug and they would walk together to the breakfast table on the east porch of the mansion, overlooking their beautiful garden with its large marble water fountain, well-manicured grass and perfectly maintained flower beds. She loved this morning time they spent together as she got the chance to enjoy a calm start for the day with a beautiful view. Sometimes an occasional butterfly would pass her by on its way to the flower beds.

The maids were instructed to prepare breakfast as decided the night before and like clockwork, it would be brought in when they arrive at the mahogany table, covered by an ivory coloured tablecloth that had golden threads decorating it.

They were in the middle of their customary peaceful breakfast when the maid brought in their mail and Arielle's outburst changed the atmosphere. She was bubbling with excitement.

"You got what? The contract?" Harold asked while cutting a piece of bacon on his plate.

"Yes!!! They want to record an album and want me to work on some original songs! That man you invited for Christmas apparently loved my new song. He thinks I have potential," Arielle couldn't believe that such an amazing opportunity was before her, but then again, wasn't she already living a life of blessing she never imagined she could have? How can she ever thank Jesus for all of this?

"I knew you'd get it," Harold replied nonchalantly as he focused on his breakfast.

Arielle felt a little let down by his apparent lack of enthusiasm for her success.

"Aren't you happy for me, Dad?"

"I am! Of course I am, Arielle! Like I said, I saw that potential in you the first time you sang in front of me... that's why I gave you a proper training," Harold smiled.

"I sense a but..." Arielle frowned.

Harold chuckled and took a sip of his tea before he focused and gave his full attention to Arielle. When he did this, Arielle knew she had to listen, because whatever came next would be important for her... even if it wasn't, she couldn't escape the piercing sharpness of Harold's eyes when his full attention was on her.

"Arielle, this is only the beginning. I'm happy you got the contract, but now comes the hard part..."

"Hard part? Like what dad?"

"The music industry isn't easy like they show it to be on TV. Writing songs that would please your recording company, getting the music right, recording the songs, marketing them and getting good sales... it takes a lot of hard work. Of course, you'll have other challenges to face... not everyone will like your music, there'll be many critiques, reporters to deal with and so on..." Harold paused to check if she was taking it all in.

She was. She understood that he was right.

"Ever since I brought you here, I tried my best to keep you at a low profile, sheltered, because I didn't want you to get hounded by the media. They can be ruthless. Every move you make will be followed... your life will never be hidden once you take such a public career. Are you ready for that?" Arielle took a moment to think.

Was she ready for this?

"You'll be with me... right, Dad?"

"Till the end."

"If I make a mess of things?"

"I'll still be there for you. That's a given, Arielle. You're my daughter. I'm never going to leave you."

"Even if you're angry with me?"

"Even if I'm angry, sad, hurt, disappointed... whatever it is, I will never give up on you Arielle. You're a Davidson remember? My child! Nothing will make me leave you."

Arielle felt her confidence rise.

"Well... if God is with me and you're also with me, I can face any challenge! I'm ready!" she smiled.

The first year was difficult for Arielle, just like Harold predicted. The producer found some fault with every song she wrote. It was difficult for her to write the eight songs required for her first album.

Then the time came to record the music and the band assigned to her wouldn't cooperate with her. They kept resisting her ideas and her approach to the song until the producer finally decided to change the band for her. That's when her past came back to haunt her. She met Nathan again.

When the new band was introduced to Arielle, she immediately recognized Nathan and she froze from shock. He stared at her when the producer introduced her as "Arielle Davidson Rodrigo" while she was engrossed observing him. Nathan was still as tall as she remembered him. Still good looking and handsome in every way. There were some changes though. His hair was slightly longer, there was a shadow of a beard and he wasn't wearing his glasses. *He must have gotten contacts*, Heather thought. Her producer interrupted her reverie and indicated that he wanted to talk to her.

"Arielle, this is a new band that we recently signed in to our company. They're relatively fresh to the industry, so they might work better with you," her producer advised, taking her aside.

Arielle nodded and as instructed, she spoke generally with the band, avoiding eye contact with Nathan and their first recording was scheduled. Once this was done, the meeting was over, and everyone rose to go but Nathan lingered. He wanted to talk to her. It was obvious, but Arielle remembered Harold's condition: "You have to leave the past behind." She was no longer the Heather Nathan knew. She was Arielle who didn't know Nathan. So, she gathered her stuff and walked out of the room.

"You're awfully quiet tonight," Harold broke the silence at the dinner table. They were seated next to each other in the large dining table which when they had company, could seat up to fourteen guests.

"No ranting about the horrid band or merciless producer today?" he pressed on. Arielle shook her head and looked resigned.

This worried Harold. He didn't like seeing Arielle upset. "Hey, what happened?"

Arielle twirled the spaghetti on her plate without making any move to eat it.

"Come-on... tell me... maybe I can help?"

Arielle sighed and looked up, her eyes shining with unshed tears.

"I saw Nathan today."

Harold started to see her potential dilemma.

"This was the boy you liked?"

"Yes... the one who hated me and never came back."

"How did you see him?"

"He's in the new band they brought in for me."

Harold was surprised at this turn of events.

"You didn't tell me he was a musician."

"He wasn't. I've never heard him play before."

"Well... clearly there were things about him that you didn't know."

"Yeah..." Arielle sighed.

"So, what happened? Did he recognize you?"

"I think he did..."

"Did he try to talk?"

"He waited while everyone else was leaving..."

"So, he did want to talk to you!" Harold grinned.

"Dad! Why are you grinning! You told me to leave my past behind and now my past is here!" Arielle broke into a sob.

"Oh honey... I'm sorry, I don't know why you're upset! I

thought you wanted to talk to this boy again?"

"I did!"

"But?"

"I didn't! Because you said to leave the past behind!" she continued to sob.

Understanding dawned on Harold.

"I didn't want you to hate me if you found out that I talked with Nathan and leave me. It was the only condition you put on me... so I didn't talk to him." Harold was touched by her loyalty to him. He quickly got up from his seat, came over to Arielle and enveloped her with a big hug.

"There, there my little girl... I'm so happy you thought of me and stopped yourself from talking to Nathan... because you didn't want me to leave you... but I told you right? No matter what you do... you're my daughter – that won't change!"

"But the condition?"

"I wanted you to leave your old identity behind – your name and so on because it was too painful for you and was unnecessary baggage for you to carry into your future with me... but that doesn't mean I don't want you to speak with the people in your past who you want in your future. I'm not that cruel you know, to keep you from things you like... that are good for you."

"So, you won't mind if I talk to him?"

"Of course I won't mind. I'll be happy you can sort things out with him. Maybe there was a reason why he couldn't come to meet you last time Arielle... from the way you described his friendship with you, I don't think he hated you."

"I'm not too sure of that, Dad."

"Well... I have a good feeling about this. Go ahead. Talk to Nathan and see what happens."

Arielle hugged Harold tightly.

"You're the best dad in the world! Seriously!"

Harold smiled lovingly at this little girl who walked into his life with such an extraordinary set of circumstances. She has firmly taken a significant place in his life.

"Okay, that's a wrap for today! Good job guys!" the producer was happy with the results. "That's a first time," Arielle thought as she took off her headphones and handed them to the assistant. She quickly walked out of the studio after thanking the band and the sound operators. Nathan received her thanks but didn't say anything. *I guess he must be mad because I left without talking last time.*

She really wanted to talk to him but didn't know how to get him to stay behind without making things awkward with the other band members. So she waited outside the studio, close to the front door.

"I'm going ahead guys! See you later!" that was Nathan's voice! He came outside, and he was alone.

Their eyes locked and Arielle's mouth went dry.

"See you, Miss Arielle!" Nathan nodded curtly before turning to walk away.

"Nathan! Wait!" She found her voice again as she hurried towards him.

"Don't you recognize me?" she asked, feeling hurt that maybe he couldn't even remember her.

Nathan's eyes softened "Of course I do... Heather..." he mumbled softly. "I thought you didn't want to talk to me."

"I do! I really do!" Heather was glad.

"I haven't told my band mates that I know you from school."

"Okay, shall we go somewhere more private and talk?"

"Sure... where do you suggest?"

"There's a library down the road," she smiled.

"For old time's sake?" Nathan grinned.

"Yeah…" she grinned back, and they started to walk when a car pulled up beside them.

It was her driver. She completely forgot the rules! "Ah! We can't walk. Let's get in the car, he'll take us."

"Tight security?" Nathan raised an eyebrow.

"Something like that," Arielle sighed. "But its fine you know, I've gotten used to it."

They pulled up at the library and Arielle instructed the driver to be back in an hour.

They walked inside the red brick building and found a private corner away from the librarian and others. It was like old times when they used to hang out at the library near Oceans International.

"Okay then," Nathan mumbled as they found some seats at a small wooden table.

Silence settled in and they looked at each other for a moment, wondering who would speak first.

"One question…" Nathan broke the silence.

"Yeah?"

"Why did you do it?" Nathan's expression was grim – like he was remembering a painful memory. Even if his beard was just a shadow, it made him look more serious. *He must be talking about the photos,* Arielle thought, feeling the old guilt return.

"Mikesh… those photos… I'm so sorry Nathan. I didn't know he was trying to take revenge on you… I know I shouldn't have tried those…" Nathan leaned over and grabbed her hand gently and interrupted her.

"I don't care about the photos…" He spoke softly, looking deep into her eyes as if the answers he searched for would be found there. "Why did you jump?" Without his glasses, it felt like his gaze could see deep into her soul. It made her a little uncomfortable even as she felt relief flood in to her. So, he didn't care about the photos after all... Harold was right. There must have been some other reason why he didn't come home during that break.

"Is it hard for you to tell me?" Nathan prodded.

"No..." Arielle took a deep breath and she told him everything that happened. She told Nathan how she felt about him leaving without a goodbye, what Bella told her when he didn't come home for holidays and she finally gave him the apology she always wanted give, for liking him. She promised him she wouldn't be a burden in his life.

Nathan listened attentively and sighed.

"So, my assumptions were right. We were both manipulated by Bella"

"Manipulated? What do you mean?"

Then it was Nathan's turn to explain to her what he found out from Mikesh and how he never hated her but always considered her as his best friend.

"When I came back and heard the news from my mom, I didn't know what to do! You were gone, and no one knew where you were, and I gave up hope on ever meeting you again!"

Arielle couldn't believe what she heard. "Wow! Thank God he rescued me! I would have died for no reason!"

"Yes! Thank God! Don't you ever do something stupid like that again!" for a brief moment, Nathan's eyes flashed in anger; "You're irreplaceable! Chamember that!"

"I won't... I know Jesus now. So, no matter how hard things get, I have hope in Jesus to keep going... because he's with me."

"You've changed," Nathan realized as he observed Arielle. "You're more confident now."

"Is that a bad thing?" Arielle grinned.

"Not at all! It's awesome! I'm happy for you!"

"It's all thanks to Dad... as in Harold..."

"The guy who adopted you?"

"Yeah..."

"Tell me about him."

So Arielle explained to him how Harold told her about Jesus in the hospital and later, after he was discharged, how he came to adopt her and changed her name.

"So how is it like? Being his daughter? He's a millionaire, right? If it's the same David Harold Rodrigo that I'm thinking of."

"Yeah..." Arielle grinned sheepishly. "I had no idea who he was until I came to his house."

Nathan looked at her in wonder. "You had no idea who he was, and you agreed to be his daughter? What were you thinking?"

"My other option was to go to an orphanage! Harold was kind to me... I didn't have any doubts."

Nathan sighed. "... and it's been good Nathan. He's very kind. He takes very good care of me and I actually feel like I have a family now... a family that loves me."

"Well... thank God it worked out well for you in the end," Nathan smiled.

A brief silence settled in until Arielle changed the subject.

"Since when did you play the guitar?" Arielle asked.

"Haven't I told you the story? Why I stopped playing the guitar?"

"No!" Arielle exclaimed.

So Nathan told her the story of his sister's death and how it made him give up on playing his guitar until he heard of Arielle's miraculous rescue from death.

"It was the talk of town when the nurse in charge of you shared it at church. Hearing the way God saved you made me examine my faith. I realized I was angry at God for what happened to my sister without realizing it was a choice she made. She chose death without turning to God for help. In fact, I think God did try to help her by getting me to plead with her that night but she wouldn't budge from the choice she made... it was sad but I couldn't blame God anymore for that... you on the other hand... you didn't even know him... and there was no one else to stop you, so He showed up and miraculously made sure you lived. I was so grateful to God for that... so I picked up my guitar again and started practicing it. Eventually I met some guys at college and we formed a band. We played some gigs at Penn State and then we came back to Colombo. One of our guys got us a manager who suggested that we upload some music videos on YouTube and then, your producer contacted us. We ended up getting a contract and then...here we are..."

"It's only God who could have orchestrated this."

"Yeah... out of all the bands out there!" Nathan chuckled

"I'm so glad! I just feel so free now, knowing the truth."

"And I'm so glad to hear that you've been doing well... I was super worried about you."

"You're always too worried about me Nathan – this needs to change now!" Arielle teased. They chuckled together.

"I hope things will go well with me and the rest of your band"

"Why? What went wrong with the previous band? Our manager said you didn't get along well with them."

"They wouldn't listen to any of my suggestions! They just did what *they* wanted and expected me to follow along with it, when its *my* song!" Arielle spoke passionately.

Nathan chuckled. "Well... you don't have to worry about that with us. My guys are very chill... and if anyone tries to trouble you, I'll take care of it! We'll make you a super star in no time!"

"Thanks, Nathan" Arielle smiled as relief eased her. "That's a huge burden off my back."

"You can count on me – anytime!"

"I know," she smiled.

"So... by the way... should I call you Heather or Arielle?"

"Arielle, please. I like it better. The company is not going to publicize the Rodrigo part on my request, so I'll be mainly known to the public as Arielle Davison"

"It's a beautiful name. Harold picked well."

"I'd like for you to meet him someday... you'd love him."

"Yeah... that'd be nice."

As they talked Arielle didn't realize how much time had passed until her mobile beeped with a message from her driver.

"Oh no! It's way past one hour!" Arielle cringed.

"Your driver is here?"

"Yeah! I hate making him wait."

"Okay... well... I'll see you at the studio then."

"Yeah for sure! Do you want me to drop you off anywhere?"

"No... I'm fine! You should get going."

"Okay then, I'll catch you later!"

They briefly hugged each other, and Arielle whispered before hurrying off "I'm so glad we met Nathan. I missed you!"

Watching her leaving, Nathan whispered, "I missed you too!"

A year later, Arielle's album was released. It did so well in sales that her name became a common household name. Everyone talked about how beautiful her songs were and many people loved them for the encouragement it gave them to face rough times. Soon her albums became popular worldwide and Arielle was able to fund orphanages and single parents using her own earnings. Arielle's dream came true. She was able to make a difference in the world through her music.

Looking back to her time as Heather, Arielle realized this success would not have been possible without the pain she endured. What Harold told her at the hospital, years ago, turned out to be true. There was a purpose hidden behind every painful experience she endured – that was the only reason why Jesus – her loving God, allowed her to go through such difficult seasons. If she didn't endure and overcome the painful seasons, she wouldn't be Arielle Davidson who brought help and hope to so many. Arielle was truly grateful for the blessings God gave her by changing her life so completely but also for the difficult times she faced. Truly, nothing was impossible for God.

EPILOGUE

"So what do you think of my little secret?" Ms. Arielle asked Jayani who was speechless. Jayani was remarkably quiet until Arielle finished telling her story.

"I'm very surprised Ms. Arielle... I never knew..."

"No one does...well, except Nathan of course"

Jayani was silent for a moment but seemed to have something on her mind.

"Do you have anything you want to ask me?" Arielle asked.

"Well... just a small question... I'm curious to know what happened to Bella, Mikesh and your parents... did you ever meet them after you became famous? Did they ever try to talk to you?"

"I haven't met Mikesh or my parents Jayani... I am very different from who I used to be... so they wouldn't recognize me now"

"Then you've met Bella?" Jayani gasped in shock. Arielle admired Jayani's sharp grasp of the information. "Yes... I did..."

"Did she recognize you? How did you meet her?" Jayani was curious.

"Do you remember the Coronavirus pandemic that shut down the world?"

"Yes! We wore masks to protect ourselves and also to stop it from spreading to others."

"Yes, that's right... well, Bella was stuck in Italy during that outbreak with no way to get back home. She was there for a business trip and asked for help on Facebook because someone had stolen her belongings. She only had a few Euros with her to survive..."

"Oh no! Was this when people were hoarding food at supermarkets?"

"Yes! There was barely any food left in stores and what was left was sold at extremely high prices. Just like the poor people who lived on daily wages, Bella would have starved if someone didn't help her come back home!"

"Well... she was so cruel to you... no wonder something bad like that happened to her!"

"I thought so too... at first... before I remembered the ways I was 'bad' myself... none of us are perfect Jayani... we all hurt other people, sometimes even the ones we love the most because of wounds and hurts we have from our past... For some reason, when Nathan told me about Bella's dilemma, I just knew I had to help her!"

"WHAT? You helped the person who pushed you to the point of suicide?" Jayani was shocked.

"Yes... I know it might seem hard to understand right now to you... She was terrible to me – yes... but knowing that I had a way to help her... it would be cruel of me to let her suffer. That wouldn't honour God. Just because she was mean to me doesn't mean I had to be cruel to her in return. Despite all my wrongs, I was loved and forgiven by Jesus so I thought maybe I should show love to her and forgive her too. So I helped her. With Harold's support, I went to Italy to bring her back..."

Jayani was surprised. "You could have caught the virus, Ms. Arielle! Why did you go that far?"

"It was a risk... but I was compelled to do it! I remembered how far Jesus went to rescue me. I placed myself in her shoes and realized she probably would need some comforting. So I got Nathan to contact her for me and met her... She was very grateful and relieved. She cried, saying how she didn't deserve the kindness I showed her because of some horrible things she did in the past. I think she regretted what happened with me... but even if she didn't, I was glad I got the chance to help her."

"Wow... I really can't believe you did that, Ms. Arielle," Jayani exhaled in disbelief.

Arielle smiled and was about to reply when out of the corner of her eyes, she saw Sharlene approaching them.

"I think I've talked to you long enough... Sharlene is coming to check on us..."

"Thank you for sharing your story with me, Ms. Arielle..."

"No problem at all... I hope you'll keep my little secret, Jayani and I really hope it will help you know that whatever you went through, you are not the only one who's had a difficult past... if I could overcome my fears and my past to be who I am today, so can you!"

With that, the life-changing encounter Jayani had with Ms. Arielle came to an end. Sharlene fussed that Jayani took up too much of Ms. Arielle's valuable time and hurriedly led Ms. Arielle away, leaving Jayani alone once again to her thoughts, which was good, because Jayani had a lot to think about.

If Ms. Arielle pushed through so much hardship to be such an amazing person today, Jayani realized that maybe she could too.

With time, Jayani overcame the memories that haunted her by choosing to focus more on the good things she had in the present. She even managed to forgive her bullies, just like Ms. Arielle forgave Bella! When things became too difficult, Jayani remembered how Jesus helped Ms. Arielle. So, likewise, Jayani asked Jesus for help and the amazing thing was, Jesus answered her prayer! Jayani wanted to be adopted and belong to a family. So she prayed and within months from the time she prayed, Jayani was in the process of getting adopted to a wonderful couple who didn't have children! They had heard her story from Sharlene and were impressed by Jayani's positive demeanour. They admired her talent in music and wanted to support her future. They chose her out of all the others in the orphanage and Jayani knew it was only because Jesus heard her when she asked for help. She was forever grateful to Ms. Arielle for sharing her story with her. It changed Jayani's outlook on life and helped her to learn about Jesus. Getting to know Jesus transformed her life. *Things will never be the same again,* Jayani thought excitedly as she looked forward to the future with her new mother and father.